INDICATE HERE WITH YOUR OWN SYMBOL
THAT YOU HAVE READ THIS BOOK
DATE DUE

GAYLORD   #3522PI   Printed in USA

The Young Man & the Sea

The Young Man & the Sea

Recipes & Crispy Fish Tales from Esca

DAVID PASTERNACK & ED LEVINE

Foreword by Mario Batali

ARTISAN

Published by Artisan
A Division of Workman Publishing, Inc.
225 Varick Street
New York, NY 10014-4381
www.artisanbooks.com

Library of Congress Cataloging-in-Publication Data

Pasternack, David.
    The young man and the sea : recipes and crispy
fish tales from Esca / David Pasternack and Ed Levine.
        p. cm.
    ISBN-13: 978-1-57965-276-0
    ISBN-10: 1-57965-276-X
    1. Cookery (Seafood) 2. Cookery, Italian. 3. Esca
(Restaurant). I. Levine, Ed, 1952– . II. Title.
TX747.P3785 2007
641.6'9—dc22   2006049235

Design by Nicholas Caruso
Printed in Singapore
First printing, April 2007

10 9 8 7 6 5 4 3 2 1

For all the fishermen who supply me
with the greatest fish in the world. —D.P.

For Vicky and Will,
the catches of my life. —E.L.

Contents

An Introductory Note

When Dave Pasternack comes out of the kitchen to talk to customers at Esca, his chef whites not so starched, stains all too readily visible on his apron, he can barely contain his enthusiasm. He tells them about the striped bass that's on the menu, which of his oddball friends caught it, how it was caught, and what's to become of the species. It was after one of my many encounters with Dave in his dining room that I decided that someone had to get Dave's stories and recipes down on paper.

I approached Dave about the idea. He had to think long and hard about whether he had the time to do it, but ultimately he decided that it would be fun and in-te-rest-ing ("interesting" in Dave-speak) to share what comes straight from his kitchen and his boat.

As you go through the book, you'll notice that Dave's style of cooking is not elaborate, difficult, or needlessly complicated. You won't find any fancy-pants, tricked-out sauces or cooking techniques in *The Young Man & the Sea*, which means a home cook will find the recipes accessible, inviting, and even empowering. Dave's food depends on great ingredients and precise cooking and seasoning. When *The New Yorker*'s Mark Singer asked Dave to describe his cooking style, he replied, "It's all about passion, plus knowing when something needs a little something."

In Dave's wake you'll find yourself thinking differently about eating fish, fishing, and life at sea or on shore. So here you have it, the wisdom and wit of David Pasternack, piscine poet, the Nietszche of the deep. Grab your fishing gear, your fry pan, and your local fishmonger. I promise you you'll never again look the same way at a piece of fish.

—Ed Levine

Foreword

It was on a trip to northeast Italy in 2000 that Dave Pasternack began to think about raw fish in a new way. Dave and I were traveling with our partner, Joe Bastianich, around the Veneto, Trieste, and the Istrian coast. It was on this trip that we were all exposed to Italian raw fish preparations. Joe coined the term *crudo* (in Italy raw fish is called *pesce crudo*, and *crudo* by itself refers to a kind of prosciutto), but Dave took that concept and made it his own. Of course we didn't know it at the time.

A few months later, right before we opened Esca, we were in the kitchen, trying this and that. Dave created a crudo that was a giant sea scallop with tangerine oil, pink peppercorns, and some Sicilian sea salt. And it was a giant moment. It was: holy mackerel (pun intended), this is gonna be a great restaurant. Now there are restaurants in every major city in America—from Portland, Oregon, to Portland, Maine—serving crudo, all because of what Dave is doing at Esca.

Dave Pasternack is the best thing to happen to Italian fish cooking in a long time. Why? Nobody knows more about fish, fishing, and fish cooking. He has an unequaled passion for all things from the deep. He lives a hundred yards from the ocean; he's out fishing when he's not cooking, and he co-owns a great fish restaurant.

When we first opened Esca, Dave would go fishing on his day off, and then bring his catch of the day into the restaurant in Manhattan on the Long Island Rail Road, in a plastic bag lined with ice. That's the kind of dedication and passion I like in friends and colleagues. That passion and dedication are reflected in the pages that follow.

What do I love about Dave? He's as pure a soul as I've met in the food world. Dave accentuates the natural and regional flavors of fish without challenging them or diminishing them. Dave thinks about Italian seafood in a whole new way. When Dave talks about the difference between the fluke in Sheepshead Bay and the fluke from some part of Long Island, you know that in fact one does taste different from the other. Dave has a real understanding of what the Italians call *materie prime*—the raw ingredients—and he does a great job making them available for any palate to explore and understand.

To Dave, sourcing is at least as important as cooking. Dave knows almost every fisherman and wholesale fishmonger from Maine to California. I wish everyone who buys this book could spend a morning with Dave at the restaurant when the phone is ringing off the hook with people telling him what they've caught that day, and purveyors are lined up outside the restaurant's door, freshly caught fish in hand, trying to get an audience with the Pope of Fish.

Dave's cooking style represents the ingredient-centric ideology that so many chefs (myself included) have adopted. His ego is not present on the plate. His food is not about Dave the chef auteur. In Dave's hands a salt-baked whole fish is a salt-baked whole fish, and the only thing that makes one better or different than the other is the fish. Isn't that refreshing? His aesthetic is so clean and clear and unmurky, much like the waters he frequently fishes in.

That's why I often have trouble deciding what to order at Esca. I always get whatever crudo Dave has come up with that day. Then a pasta, maybe the maccheroni with sea urchin and crabmeat, or the paccheri with tuna meatballs. After the pasta, maybe the lobster with chiles and mint, or a salt-baked fish, or perhaps the red snapper. It's hard to choose because Dave's food is inherently logical and unfailingly delicious, and that's why food lovers everywhere should rejoice. Because now you'll be able to cook in the comfort of your own home the dishes that Dave dazzles his customers with at Esca. All you need is a good fishmonger and/or a fishing pole, and a copy of *The Young Man & the Sea*.

I've been a friend, colleague, and admirer of Dave for more than fifteen years now. I've hung out, cooked, eaten, and drunk with him for more nights than I can remember. Dave's an original, a one-of-a-kind soul who never shrinks from telling the truth, on the plate or at the table. When you pick up a copy of *The Young Man & the Sea,* you'll get to know the same decent, straightforward, and extraordinarily talented guy I met at the Union Square greenmarket all those years ago. He's a guy's guy who understands that most of the time, a freshly caught fish is just a fish, to be enjoyed and savored with a couple of buddies and a bottle of good vino.

—Mario Batali

Introduction

I think my dad took me fishing shortly after I learned to walk. Seriously. We went out in a boat that his friend Captain Lou kept in Freeport, Long Island. Mostly we caught bluefish, but occasionally snapper or flounder. Captain Lou was one of these guys who never, ever changed his facial expression. I always fished with older guys who would take me under their wing. They would help me with my bait, my rod and reel, anything I needed to know. One thing I learned right off the bat is if you want to catch a lot of fish, you've gotta take an aggressive approach. And what's the point of fishing if you don't want to catch a lot of fish? Like my friend Mike says, "I hate fishing, but I love catching."

Even when I went to culinary school in Rhode Island, I would drive down every weekend to fish near my hometown, Rockville Centre, which was a couple of miles from the ocean. Come to think of it, I've never really lived more than five miles from the ocean. After I started working and living in Manhattan, I'd rent a room close to the beach so I could fish with my buddies on my days off. (Eventually I bought a house even closer to the water.) We'd fish the whole Atlantic Ocean (at least it seemed that way), anywhere from the Rockaways to Montauk Point. We fished for anything that swam. A couple of times I ended up catching a shark. That wasn't easy. But fishing is how I came to know and love fish. *The New Yorker*'s Mark Singer pointed out something about the similarities between writers and chefs that's always stuck with me: Writers write what they know. I guess it's the same with chefs. You cook what you know.

Most chefs get their fish from one supplier. I have bought fish from probably a hundred guys altogether. I'm always looking for new stuff. Tommy's my crab guy, Mike's my cod guy, I got guys all over the country fishing for me. I call them, they call me. That's part of the fun of my job, getting to know all these nutty guys with the same passion I have.

That's one of the reasons I love fish and fishing and cooking fish. There's always something new to learn. Someone's always calling me about some fish I've never heard of. There are too many fish in the sea, so I'll never run out of new stuff to cook with and fish for.

I love everything about fishing, from catching them, cleaning them, and butchering them to filleting them, deboning them, cooking them, you name it. I love getting to know the fat content of a fish by feeling it. Fish fat is not like animal fat, like beef or pork fat where you see inches of it around the flesh. It's something that's part of the flesh of the fish, and it adds immeasurably to the flavor each fish has. Fat is something intrinsic in fish, like the marbling of beef, and the more natural fat a fish has, the better it tastes.

Experience more than cooking school has taught me what I know about cooking fish. My experience dictates that you understand certain things about certain ingredients at certain times of year. I hope you'll learn how I think about food—how flavors work, how you have to take into consideration acidity, texture, the properties of various oils, how certain fish marry well with different herbs or vegetables. I hope that by using *The Young Man & the Sea* you'll learn to love cooking and eating fish as much as I do.

I know a lot of people think that fish is something to be scared of. So they cook only with what I call the Big 3—tuna, salmon, and swordfish—a few times a year. I've never understood that. To me, there are so many different kinds of fish with different flavors and different textures, and when you add a little something to them you end up with something you really look forward to eating. I hope you end up thinking, as I do, that cooking and eating all kinds of fish are two of life's greatest pleasures.

—Dave Pasternack

The Young Man & the Sea

Starters, Salads, Soups, & Stews

Mackerel
with White-Bean Bruschetta

This is our "welcome" dish at Esca, one that all diners receive gratis shortly after they are seated. I thought I would make it our "welcome" recipe for the book, because this easy, inexpensive dish is a great introduction to everything I serve as well as every recipe in this book. The creamy beans combine beautifully with the rich, full-flavored fish to create a dish that is earthy and satisfying, and smacks of the sea. **Makes 12 to 16 bruschetta; serves 6**

2 cups White Beans (recipe follows)

¾ cup preserved mackerel, slightly broken up (see Ingredient Notes; see Sources, page 237)

½ small red onion, finely diced, (about ⅓ cup)

⅓ cup Sicilian green olives, pitted and chopped

3 tablespoons flat-leaf parsley, roughly chopped

Juice of 1 lemon (about 3 tablespoons)

¼ cup extra-virgin olive oil, plus high-quality extra-virgin olive oil, for drizzling (see Ingredient Notes; see Sources, page 237)

¾ teaspoon sea salt, plus more to finish (see Ingredient Notes; see Sources, page 237)

Freshly ground black pepper, plus more to finish

1 baguette, cut into ¾-inch-thick slices

In a large bowl, mix together the cooked beans, mackerel, onion, olives, parsley, and lemon juice. Drizzle in the ¼ cup olive oil, season to taste, and stir gently to combine. Refrigerate for about 2 hours so the flavors integrate. Remove from the refrigerator a half hour before serving to remove some of the chill.

Grill the baguette slices over a charcoal fire or brown in a toaster oven.

To serve, spoon the bean-mackerel mixture over the warm baguette slices and arrange on a serving platter. Drizzle extra-virgin olive oil (use a squeeze bottle) over each, then finish with a sprinkling of additional sea salt and freshly ground black pepper.

INGREDIENT NOTES

You can use canned white beans (I like the Bush brand) if you don't want to go to the trouble of soaking and cooking the dried variety.

If mackerel isn't your thing, use Italian tuna canned in olive oil (see page 19) instead.

For cooking, you can use any good everyday extra-virgin olive oil, such as Colavita. But use a higher-quality oil when you drizzle it to finish a dish; I use Sicilian oil for these purposes, but there are plenty of others to choose from.

I use Sicilian sea salt at Esca. I like its natural flavor, its not overly coarse texture, and the way it sticks to food.

White Beans Serves 4

2 cups dried white beans, preferably corona, soaked overnight (see Ingredient Notes)

1 stalk celery, cut into 3 pieces

1 carrot, peeled and cut into 3 pieces

½ small white onion, roughly chopped

2 sprigs thyme

1 bay leaf

Preheat the oven to 300°F.

Using an ovenproof Dutch oven, trace the diameter of the pot onto a piece of parchment paper. Then cut out the circle and set aside. Place the beans, celery, carrot, onion, thyme, and bay leaf in the pot and fill with enough water to cover by at least 2 inches. Bring to a boil over a high flame. Turn off the flame, lay the reserved parchment circle on the surface of the beans, and cover with the lid.

Transfer to the oven and cook for approximately 1½ hours, until the beans are creamy and tender. In the oven, the beans should gently simmer. (If they boil, reduce the oven temperature.)

Set the cooked beans on the stove top to cool in their liquid. Then drain in a colander, discard the bay leaf, and rinse with cool water. The beans can be stored, covered, in the refrigerator overnight.

Fennel and Blood Orange Salad with Shrimp

This very Italian salad is a wonderful way to wake up anyone's taste buds. The fennel gives a licorice flavor and some crunch, and the blood oranges lend a spicy, juicy sweetness. A few oil-cured olives add a layer of brininess, and the arugula gives just the right hint of pepperiness. If you can't find blood oranges, tangerine sections will do just fine. This salad tastes great with or without the shrimp. In fact, you see it in trattorias all over Sicily without any fish or meat added. **Serves 4**

4 blood oranges

1 pound large shrimp (about 20), shells on, split down the back, vein removed

Sea salt

Freshly ground black pepper

½ cup plus 2 tablespoons extra-virgin olive oil

1 large fennel bulb, outer layer removed, halved, cored, and very thinly sliced (preferably shaved on a mandolin)

4 cups baby arugula, rinsed and spun dry

Use a large chef's knife to cut the tops and bottoms off the oranges. One at a time, stand each orange on a cutting board, and cut the peel away in wide strips from top to bottom. When all of the peel has been removed, cut the oranges into ⅓-inch slices, in a bowl to catch the juice. Set aside.

Season the shrimp with salt and pepper. Heat 3 tablespoons of the olive oil in a large, well-seasoned cast-iron pan over medium-high flame. In two batches, cook the shrimp for 2 minutes per side. They should be opaque, with crispy shells. Transfer the cooked shrimp to a plate and set aside (this can be done up to 2 hours ahead and held at room temperature). When they're cool enough to handle, peel the shrimp.

In a mixing bowl, combine the saved fennel and arugula. Season with an additional ½ teaspoon salt and a few turns of freshly ground black pepper. Add the sliced oranges along with their juice and the remaining 4 tablespoons olive oil, and use your hands to toss. Divide the salad among four shallow serving bowls. Toss the shrimp in the dressing that remains in the bottom of the mixing bowl, and then top the salads with them. Give each bowl a light sprinkling of sea salt and freshly ground black pepper before serving.

INGREDIENT NOTE

Although I like to dig into a plate of shrimp, shells and all, I realize that most people don't want to go to the trouble of wrestling with the shells before they pop a shrimp into their mouth. So the recipe calls for peeling the shrimp before serving them.

Puntarelle Salad

When I was visiting Italy fifteen years ago with a friend, I ate this amazing veal with puntarelle in a little trattoria. When I got back to the States, I vowed to use puntarelle in my own cooking. Puntarelle is the quintessential Italian fall bitter green, a cross between dandelion and chicory with a pronounced fennel flavor. If you can't find puntarelle, by all means use chicory, escarole, or even romaine.

The anchovy vinaigrette lends a salty counterpoint to the bitter puntarelle, but by soaking the anchovies beforehand you remove any excessive saltiness. In a Roman trattoria this is served as an accompaniment to saltimbocca, the classic preparation of veal with ham and cheese. **Serves 4**

½ loaf brick-oven or any hearty bread

1 cup olive oil

1 teaspoon sea salt

½ teaspoon freshly ground black pepper

10 tinned anchovies (preferably Recca brand; see Sources, page 237)

3 tablespoons white-wine vinegar

Juice of 1 lemon

1 head puntarelle, leaves split, well rinsed, and spun dry

4 marinated white anchovies (sold by your fishmonger)

Preheat the oven to 325°F.

Remove and discard the crusts from the loaf. Dice the bread into ½-inch cubes (you should have about 1½ cups). Place the cubes on a baking tray and drizzle with ¼ cup of the olive oil, the salt and pepper. Toss to coat. Bake, shaking the tray occasionally, until the croutons are crisp and golden brown, 15 to 20 minutes. These can be made the day before and stored in a paper bag overnight.

In a blender, combine the tinned anchovies, vinegar, lemon juice, and ½ cup water. Pulse to combine. With the blender running on a medium speed, add the remaining olive oil in a slow, steady stream until the mixture emulsifies to a creamy dressing.

In a mixing bowl, drizzle the puntarelle with the anchovy dressing. Use your hands to toss. Divide the dressed leaves among four serving plates and top each plate with one marinated anchovy. Serve immediately.

INGREDIENT NOTES

If you don't love the flavor of anchovies, feel free to halve the number called for in the recipe. This is a salad you have to overdress, because the dressing acts as a sauce that moistens the entire dish.

Seafood Salad
Esca

I had the greatest seafood salad ever in Amalfi at Zaccaria, a restaurant that was built on the cliffs around sidewalks that snaked through the town. So between bites I found myself dodging kids riding their bikes and kicking soccer balls right in the middle of the trattoria. Seafood salad is always a great summer dish, and this version is made up of my ideal combination: calamari, scallops, scungilli, mussels, and shrimp. I slice the calamari and scungilli, but leave the shrimp whole because people love to see big shrimp—if you're spending money on the good stuff, why chop it up? Let the salad sit for about an hour so the flavors meld, and then serve it at room temperature or even a little warm. Chilling it causes everything to stiffen up, and it's never as delicious. Serve it on a big platter, family-style, of course. **Serves 4**

3 dried mild red chiles (such as Italian finger hots)

Three 3-inch-long strands seaweed (optional; ask your fishmonger)

Zest of 2 lemons

2 tablespoons sea salt, plus more to finish

¾ pound scungilli (see Ingredient Note; optional, see Sources, page 237)

½ pound sea scallops, muscle removed, each sliced horizontally into 4 pieces

½ pound calamari (optional)

1 pound large shrimp, peeled and deveined

1 pound cultivated mussels in shells, scrubbed (discard any with open shells)

¾ cup extra-virgin olive oil

3 large cloves garlic, thinly sliced

Juice of 3 lemons (about ½ cup)

¼ cup red-wine vinegar

1 small red onion, cut into a small dice

⅓ cup flat-leaf parsley leaves, minced, plus 6 sprigs, for garnish

⅓ cup mint leaves, minced, plus additional leaves, for garnish

1 teaspoon red pepper flakes

Freshly ground black pepper, to finish

Place the dried chiles, seaweed, and half the lemon zest in a 6-quart pot filled with four quarts of water. Bring to a boil over high heat, then reduce the heat to low and simmer for 20 minutes. Add the 2 tablespoons sea salt.

If using scungilli, add them to the simmering broth and cook for about 5 minutes, until they are tender (test by biting them). Remove with a slotted spoon, drain, and set aside in a large mixing bowl. When cool enough to handle, thinly slice.

continued

If you're not using scungilli, begin by adding the scallops to the broth and simmer for 1 minute, until the flesh is opaque. Remove with a slotted spoon, drain, and add to the large bowl. Add the calamari, if you are using it, and cook for 1 minute, then transfer to the large bowl with a slotted spoon. Cook the shrimp for 2 minutes, until they are just opaque; remove, drain, and place in the bowl. Finally cook the mussels for 4 to 5 minutes, until their shells begin to open. Remove the mussels with a slotted spoon and set aside on a separate plate from the other cooked seafood. Discard any mussels that haven't opened.

In a small skillet over a medium flame, heat 2 tablespoons of the oil until it shimmers. Add the garlic and cook, stirring occasionally, until softened but not brown, about 2 minutes. Pour the contents of the pan over the cooked seafood. Add the remaining olive oil and lemon zest, and the lemon juice, vinegar, onion, minced parsley, minced mint, and red pepper flakes. Fold in to thoroughly combine the ingredients. Add the mussels still in their shells, gently fold in, and cover the bowl with foil. Set aside at room temperature for 1 hour to let the flavors meld.

Toss the ingredients and season to taste with salt and pepper before spooning onto a large serving platter. Bruise the mint leaves and parsley sprigs for the garnish between your fingers and sprinkle on top.

INGREDIENT NOTE

If scungilli or calamari aren't your thing, leave them out and compensate with other seafood. Just using shrimp and scallops will result in an equally delicious dish.

Tentacles

Most people are weirded out by the thought of buying or cooking anything with tentacles. But if you understand what each tentacled species is and how to prepare it, you'll find that cooking these leggy wonders is actually easy and fun.

- **Calamari** is squid. No matter what they're called and what size they are, calamari have ten tentacles. Buy the small ones that smell like the ocean. I use the tentacles as well as the head of the squid: Remove the tentacles as one whole piece by slicing off just above where they begin. Slice the body into ½-inch rings. Use your fingers to pull the cartilage out of the head and continue slicing.

- **Cuttlefish** is another cephalopod that looks like a big squid. It also has ten legs, and most people think cuttlefish is the most tender of the tentacled species. I often use the ink from the cuttlefish in pasta preparations.

- **Octopus.** Although a giant octopus can have 50-foot-long tentacles, most octopuses have eight tentacles that are 1 to 2 feet long. Octopuses generally weigh between 2 and 3 pounds.

- **Scungilli** is the Italian word for channeled or knobbed whelks. A whelk is a large sea snail in the gastropod family. You often see other kinds of whelk, known as common or waved whelk, on seafood platters called *plats du mer* served in French restaurants. Scungilli is usually sold out of its shell and lightly precooked.

Baccalà Salad

My grandmother, a great one-pot cook who owned a family-style restaurant in Coney Island, loved salt cod. With good reason. As Mark Kurlansky wrote in his book *Cod*, this fish changed the world. People from all over the globe came to the waters of the North Atlantic in search of cod, and when they did find it, they needed a way to preserve it. And that's how baccalà (salt cod) came into being. There are two keys to ensuring the success of this warm salad: the quality of the baccalà you purchase, and handling it properly. There are no shortcuts in making baccalà: you have to soak it for 3 days, and you have to change the water often. **Serves 4**

1 pound boneless salt cod (see Sources, page 237), cut into 3-inch chunks

1 medium yellow onion, cut into a large dice

1 leek, damaged outer leaves discarded, cut into 3-inch pieces, rinsed thoroughly

1 stalk celery, cut into 3-inch pieces

1 bay leaf

½ cup dry white wine

1 crispy tart apple, such as Crispin or Northern Spy

½ tablespoon lemon juice

½ pound fingerling potatoes (about 7)

Salt

4 scallions, sliced thinly on the diagonal

2 tablespoons red-wine vinegar

3 tablespoons high-quality extra-virgin olive oil

Freshly ground black pepper

½ cup loosely packed flat-leaf parsley, for garnish

Place the cod in a large bowl and add enough water to cover by 3 inches. Refrigerate for 3 days, rinsing and changing the water twice per day. On day 3, give the cod a final rinse and set aside.

Place the onion, leek, celery, bay leaf, and wine in a large pot. Add 3 quarts water and bring to a boil over a high flame. Reduce the heat to low and simmer for 20 minutes. Strain and discard the vegetables, then return the broth to the pot.

Set the heat so the aromatic broth is barely simmering. Add the salt cod and slowly poach for 1 to 1½ hours, until the fish is tender and beginning to flake. Remove the pot from the flame, and refrigerate the salt cod in the poaching liquid overnight.

The next day, remove the salt cod with a slotted spoon and pat the pieces dry with paper towels. Pull off the skin, then pull out any pinbones that you find. Set aside.

Peel and dice the apple, giving the diced pieces a squirt of fresh lemon juice so they don't turn brown.

Place the potatoes in a 2-quart pot and add enough water to cover by at least 3 inches. Bring to a boil over a high flame, salt the water, and cook the potatoes until they are easily pierced with a paring knife, about 10 minutes. Drain. When cool enough to handle, peel the potatoes and cut into $1/3$-inch rounds. Place in a mixing bowl along with the apples and scallions. Break the salt cod into large flakes into the bowl. Drizzle in the vinegar, olive oil, and pepper to taste, and toss gently to combine. Season to taste with salt (the saltiness of the baccalà will vary, so taste the mixture before seasoning it).

Serve the baccalà at room temperature, garnished with the parsley.

INGREDIENT NOTE

High-quality salt cod is salted on the bone with sea salt, keeping the flesh moist and turning it slightly gray. In many markets dried salt cod is labeled *bacalao*, which is just the Spanish name for baccalà

Grilled Tuna
with Artichoke Salad

One winter my partner "Molto" (Mario Batali) took me to the Amalfi Coast to see how the chefs cook fish, and it was there that I fell in love with serving fish with raw artichokes. Artichokes in Italy seem to taste better. They have a more distinct earthy flavor, and the hearts over there are creamier. Raw artichokes are very light, have a great deal of acidity, and are slightly bitter, all of which helps cut through the richness of the tuna. Two things ensure the success of the dish: using the best tuna you can afford, and using fresh artichokes. **Serves 4**

1 large fennel bulb, outer layer removed, cored, and very thinly sliced (preferably using a mandolin)

4 cups baby arugula, rinsed and spun dry

2 lemons

8 small artichokes (or 4 large)

Four 6-ounce tuna steaks, about 1¾ to 2 inches thick

6 tablespoons extra-virgin olive oil, plus high-quality extra-virgin olive oil, for drizzling

Sea salt

Freshly ground black pepper

In a mixing bowl, combine the sliced fennel and the arugula. Set aside.

Squeeze one of the lemons into another mixing bowl filled with water. Working with one artichoke at a time, peel away the lower toughest leaves. Cut off the top third (down to the heart) using a heavy chef's knife. Place the artichoke on its side on a cutting board and cut away the leaves all the way around to reveal the heart. Remove the stem. Use a paring knife to peel and clean the heart, giving a smooth and clean appearance. Use a spoon to scoop out the fibrous inside of the heart (the thistle), and then thinly slice the cleaned heart, transferring the slices into the acidulated water. Repeat with the remaining artichokes.

Preheat an outdoor grill or grill pan to a high heat.

Rub the tuna steaks with some of the 6 tablespoons olive oil and season both sides with salt and pepper.

In a medium bowl, combine the juice of the other lemon and the remainder of the 6 tablespoons olive oil. Season with salt and pepper. Set this dressing aside.

When the coals are white-hot, place the fish over the medium-high part of the fire (where you can hold your hand above the coals for, say, 4 seconds). If the flames jump to touch the fish, move it to a cooler part of the grill. Grill the fish for 3 to 4 minutes per side. When finished, the fish should have a firmness similar to the fleshy part of your palm.

Drain the artichokes and combine with the reserved fennel and arugula. Add the reserved dressing and toss well. Divide the salad among four serving plates and top each with a tuna steak. Drizzle with a high-quality extra-virgin olive oil and serve immediately.

Dave's Tuna Advice

There's a lot of tuna out there, so I want to explain the different species you might encounter. No matter what kind of tuna you buy, make sure it doesn't have too many veins or ribbons of exposed cartilage. If you see veins, that means it wasn't bled correctly. Sometimes you see a rainbow effect on the flesh, which is not desirable. Tuna is a warm-blooded fish, so the more energy it expends when being caught, the less fat it has.

- **Albacore (long-fin)** is what is used in most canned tuna fish. It can have white or red flesh, and is the first tuna that shows up in the North Atlantic around June. Albacore is fished up and down the East Coast, from the Gulf of Texas to the Gulf of Maine. It has a coarse texture and is quite fatty. It's a very tasty fish.

- **Bonita** is also called in-shore tuna because it's caught along the beaches. Bonita is oilier than albacore with mahogany red flesh. It has a very rich, minerally flavor. Some people would call that fishy. I use it for crudo, and it makes great sushi.

- **Blackfin,** a Southern fish, is also called small school tuna. It's pretty hard to find, even for me. Blackfin tuna has a very clean taste, with amber red flesh. Again, it's a great fish to use in crudo preparations.

- **Big eye** is an expensive species beloved by the Japanese. It has a minerally, beefy flavor with plenty of fat and flesh a vibrant red color. Big eye is prized and fished for all over the world.

- **Bluefin** is the Rolls-Royce of tuna, very expensive. It ranges in color from dark to bright red. A bluefin can weigh from a hundred to a thousand pounds. The most prized bluefin are from the North Atlantic.

- **Yellowfin** is the most common of all tuna, caught the world over year-round. Yellowfin flesh ranges from cream to bright red. It's a great tuna to use for sashimi or crudo.

Grilled Sardines with Caponata

There are probably as many recipes for caponata as there are cooks in Italy. But many caponatas are too sweet, too greasy, or too vinegary. Caponata is a condiment, and all recipes for it are based on eggplant, but a good caponata has to have some texture; it can't be mush. And there should be layers of flavor: sweet, tangy, salty, nutty. I love caponata with grilled fresh sardines, which have a nutty taste and are strong enough to stand up to the caponata's flavors. In this dish, each bite is a little different: you get an olive, you get a caper, you get a raisin, you get a nut. It's interesting food. And it won't cost you a fortune. Make the caponata the day before. It can be served hot or cold or at room temperature. **Serves 4**

2 medium eggplant (about 2 pounds), peeled and cut into ½-inch cubes (if using young small eggplants, leave them unpeeled)

Sea salt

⅓ cup plus 2 tablespoons olive oil, plus additional for coating the sardines

1 clove garlic, thinly sliced

½ small onion, diced

1 bay leaf

15 Gaeta olives, pitted and halved

2 tablespoons light brown sugar

1 tablespoon capers

1 tablespoon raisins

1 tablespoon pine nuts

⅓ cup balsamic vinegar

Freshly ground black pepper

16 fresh sardine fillets (see Ingredient Notes)

High-quality extra-virgin olive oil, for drizzling

Place the cubed eggplant in a colander or on a cooling rack over a sheet pan. Sprinkle liberally with salt. Let sit for at least 2 hours.

Use paper towels to dry the eggplant and brush away the salt. Heat ⅓ cup of the olive oil in a deep, straight-sided sauté pan over a medium-high flame. Add the eggplant and, using a spatula to stir, cook for 5 minutes, until limp and tender. Transfer the cooked eggplant back to the colander to drain.

Heat the 2 tablespoons of oil in the same pan over a medium flame. Add the garlic and let it infuse for about a minute. Add the diced onion and the bay leaf. Cook until the onion is translucent, about 3 minutes. Add the olives, brown sugar, capers, raisins, pine nuts, and balsamic vinegar. Stir to combine. Add the reserved eggplant,

continued

continuing to stir gently. Cook until the pan is almost dry, about 5 minutes. Season with salt and pepper, transfer to a bowl, and set aside until the caponata is room temperature, or refrigerate overnight.

Prepare a charcoal fire or preheat the broiler.

Brush the sardines with olive oil and season each side with salt and pepper. Grill, skin side down, over white-hot coals (or skin side up under a broiler) for 1 to 2 minutes to char the skin; cook on skin side only.

To serve, spoon some caponata onto four serving plates. Top each with four grilled sardines, skin side up. Finish with a drizzle of high-quality extra-virgin olive oil, a little sea salt, and some freshly ground black pepper.

INGREDIENT NOTES

The only trick to sardines is buying them fresh. We get sardines imported from Europe. You can't get them every day, so when you see them in the market it pays to buy them. They have to be a shiny silver, with bright eyes, and their bellies broken. Have them gutted by your fishmonger. You don't have to worry about scales because sardines lose them, for some reason, as soon as they come out of the water.

Buy small eggplant; they have fewer seeds.

Sautéed Scallops
with Tomato Vinaigrette

This tomato vinaigrette is really just a vine-ripened Brandywine tomato puree mixed with a little sherry vinegar and olive oil. You can use any vine-ripened tomatoes in this dish, but I like Brandywines because they puree very well. Watch the scallops like a hawk when you're sautéing them, as they go from succulent to tirelike in an instant. Make sure the sea scallops you buy are dry scallops (not treated with sodium phosphate; see page 64). **Serves 4 as an appetizer**

FOR THE TOMATO VINAIGRETTE

½ pound Brandywine or beefsteak tomatoes

1 tablespoon sherry vinegar

3 tablespoons extra-virgin olive oil

1 teaspoon sea salt

½ teaspoon freshly ground black pepper

¼ cup mixed basil leaves, roughly chopped

FOR THE SCALLOPS

1 pound sea scallops (about 12)

Sea salt

Freshly ground black pepper

3 tablespoons extra-virgin olive oil

3 tablespoons butter, broken into 12 pieces

MAKE THE TOMATO VINAIGRETTE

Bring a large pot of salted water to a boil. Score the bottom of each tomato with an X and then drop them into the water. Blanch for about 4 minutes; you'll see the skin start to curl where the X is. Remove from the water. When cool enough to handle, cut them in half through the stem end, peel off the skins, and gently squeeze out the seeds. Discard the skins and seeds. Cut out the core.

Place the tomatoes in a blender along with the vinegar, olive oil, salt, and pepper. Puree briefly—the mixture should be nearly smooth. Add the basil and pulse for a second or two to combine.

MAKE THE SCALLOPS AND SERVE

Dry the scallops with paper towels and season both sides with salt and pepper.

Heat the olive oil in a large, preferably nonstick, sauté pan over a medium-high flame until smoking. Place the scallops in the pan, top each with a piece of butter, and cook, undisturbed, for about 3 minutes before turning them (they should caramelize on each side to a crisp golden brown).

Serve the scallops in shallow bowls with the Tomato Vinaigrette spooned over. Eat with a spoon.

Poached Gulf Shrimp and Heirloom Tomato Salad

The cooks in my kitchen always kid me that this is my version of a steakhouse shrimp cocktail. But it's better, because in steakhouses they tend to overcook the inferior-quality shrimp they use in the dish. Everyone loves a shrimp cocktail when it is prepared properly. Gulf shrimp are the most common variety found in this country (see opposite page). They come in many different sizes (the bigger ones are more expensive), and for this dish I like to use jumbo shrimp, because they look great next to the sliced tomatoes. **Serves 4**

1 lemon, halved

Sea salt

1 stalk celery

1 small yellow onion, halved

1/2 fennel bulb, roughly chopped

2 large or 3 medium (4-inch) basil stems (not the leaves), plus 1/4 cup basil leaves (preferably lemon basil)

1 tablespoon black peppercorns

1 pound jumbo shrimp, shelled and deveined

2 pounds heirloom tomatoes (Brandywine, Green Marvill, Yellow Taxis—mix 'em up) or vine-ripened tomatoes

1 cucumber, peeled, seeded, and diced

1/2 cup to 3/4 cup Sherry Vinaigrette (recipe follows)

Freshly ground black pepper

In a large pot, combine 2 quarts of water with the lemon halves, 2 teaspoons salt, the celery, onion, fennel, basil stems, and peppercorns. Bring to a boil over a high flame. Reduce to a simmer.

Add the shrimp to the court bouillon and poach until they just turn pink, 2 to 3 minutes. Use a slotted spoon to transfer the shrimp to a sheet pan lined with paper towels.

Core and slice the tomatoes (wedge, dice, or slice according to their size). Put the tomatoes in a colander over a bowl and let sit for 10 minutes to drain. Transfer the tomatoes to a mixing bowl and add the cucumber, cooked shrimp, and basil leaves. Dress with the Sherry Vinaigrette, season with salt and pepper, and toss gently to combine.

Divide the salad among four wide, shallow bowls, distributing the shrimp evenly.

EQUIPMENT NOTE

A shrimp deveiner is one of those great little kitchen tools that I for one couldn't live without. It removes the shrimp's intestine in one easy stroke.

Sherry Vinaigrette Makes ¾ cup

3 tablespoons sherry-wine vinegar

1½ teaspoons lemon juice

2¼ teaspoons Dijon mustard

½ teaspoon sea salt

¼ teaspoon freshly ground black pepper

½ cup extra-virgin olive oil

In a small mixing bowl, whisk together the sherry vinegar, lemon juice, mustard, salt, and pepper. Add the olive oil in a slow, steady stream while whisking until emulsified. The dressing can be made ahead and refrigerated; whisk before serving.

Dave's Shrimp Advice

- At Esca I use only fresh wild shrimp of all kinds, from the Carolinas or Georgia or Louisiana or Texas if they're Gulf shrimp, or Key West shrimp (see headnote, page 130), or ruby red Maine shrimp (see headnote, page 60) or their West Coast counterpart, spot prawns, which are very perishable and delicious and beloved by the Japanese, which is why we see so few of them on the East Coast. On page 237 you'll find sources for all these shrimp.

- In your local fish market you're likely to see mostly farmed Gulf-style shrimp that are frozen immediately after they're harvested. Shrimp farming has become a huge business all over the world, from Vietnam to South Africa. These shrimp can be delicious as long as you buy them from someone who knows how to handle them. Look at the shrimp. Do they glisten? Does their ice bed look as though it is replenished frequently? The shrimp shouldn't be oozing anything. They should look like they could stand at attention on their own if they stood up. They should look pristine, not dreary, not like they could use a cold shower.

- People like the prestige and the wow factor associated with serving and eating big shrimp, but the smaller ones can have just as much flavor.

- If the shrimp have black tails, don't buy them, because the black tails mean they're past their prime.

- Buy shrimp in the shell if you can, with the head intact. The head holds a lot of flavor that is lost when the shrimp is beheaded.

Ventresca Tuna Salad

I like rare seared tuna as much as the next guy, but I find it doesn't have the complex flavor I yearn to taste in tuna. Instead, I cook tuna slowly in olive oil and let it marinate as it cools. It's thoroughly cooked, but if you do it the right way, it's still rich enough to melt in your mouth. I like to keep the tuna chunky, not break it up too much, and toss it into a salad served on a big platter. No matter how I plan to serve the tuna, I first cut it into chunks and season it with sea salt and pepper. Cooking tuna this way is like making pot roast: if you make it on Monday and wait until Wednesday to eat it, it will only be better. The Italians have done tuna that way for a thousand years: they'd catch the tuna when it was running in the Strait of Messina, and preserve it in oil.

I often put the cooked tuna in oil and seal it in canning jars, but you can refrigerate it for a few days. Just bring it to room temperature before you use it. You can even serve it warm—chunks of it over spaghetti with black olives and some of the oil. Or with a white bean salad. Or over ripe tomatoes. But the important thing to remember is that tuna cooked this way is no good piping hot or ice cold. **Serves 4**

1½ pounds fresh tuna, preferably yellowfin or albacore belly cut (see Ingredient Notes)

Sea salt

Freshly ground black pepper

2 large cloves garlic, smashed

1¼ cups extra-virgin olive oil (plus additional if using salt-packed anchovies)

3 sprigs lemon thyme (or plain thyme, plus 1 teaspoon lemon zest)

2 bay leaves

4 large salted anchovies, preferably Agostino Recca brand, or 8 anchovies packed in oil (see Ingredient Notes)

¾ pound fingerling potatoes

1 pound fresh green beans, stemmed

1 small red onion, very thinly sliced (preferably using a mandolin)

½ cup flat-leaf parsley leaves, coarsely chopped

¼ cup lovage or inner leaves from celery, coarsely chopped

¼ cup red-wine vinegar, preferably Chianti

Cut the tuna into 1½-inch chunks. Season well with salt and pepper. Place in a saucepan with the garlic and add 1 cup of the oil, so the tuna is just covered (adjust the olive oil amount if necessary). Over a low flame, bring to a gentle simmer and cook for 10 minutes, taking care that the oil does not boil. Remove the pan from the heat. Add the lemon thyme and bay leaves, and set aside to cool to room temperature. The tuna can be used at this point, but will be better if allowed to marinate. Transfer the contents of the pan to a medium bowl, cover, and refrigerate overnight. Bring to room temperature at least an hour before serving.

Soak the salt-packed anchovies in water for 2 hours and drain. Remove the bones, cut anchovies into ½-inch pieces, and toss with a little olive oil. (Or drain the oil-packed anchovies and cut them into pieces.)

Place the potatoes in a pot of salted water, bring to a boil, and cook until tender, about 10 minutes. Drain. When cool enough to handle, peel and halve lengthwise. Place in a large bowl.

Meanwhile, bring 6 quarts of salted water to a boil, and prepare a bowl of ice water. Add the beans to the water and cook until tender, 5 to 7 minutes. Drain and place in the ice water. When cool, drain again and pat dry on paper towels. Add the cooked beans to the bowl with the potatoes along with the anchovies, onion, parsley, and lovage. Drain the tuna, reserving the oil. Break the pieces of fish into smaller pieces, and add to the bowl.

In a small bowl, beat the vinegar with the remaining ¼ cup olive oil and ¼ cup of the tuna's cooking oil. Season with additional salt and pepper, then pour the dressing over the tuna and beans. Toss gently but thoroughly. Serve in wide shallow bowls.

INGREDIENT NOTES

I prefer yellowfin or albacore tuna, and I use the belly cut (*ventresca* in Italian) because it's the fattiest; regular canned tuna comes from the shoulder. In some grocery stores (see Sources, page 237) you can buy canned tuna that's labeled ventresca. If you don't have access to good fresh tuna or don't have the time, feel free to substitute canned ventresca instead of cooking it yourself. But don't use regular canned tuna for this dish; it will be too dry and mealy.

The recipe calls for salted anchovies. I soak them to get rid of some of the salt, but you need something salty in the dish to make it work. If you're not an anchovy eater, substitute another salty food. Some nice Calabrese olives with their anise flavor will do the trick. Or a few big capers.

Marinated Sardines
with Roasted Eggplant

Eggplant goes really well with fresh sardines because its mild, neutral flavor is able to take on the big taste of the marinated sardines. (This dish cannot be made with salted anchovies, which can be used only as a flavoring or seasoning.) I like to use small eggplant because they tend to have fewer seeds and they're not as bitter. When you roast eggplant as you would peppers, over an open flame, it develops a smoky flavor that I love. **Serves 4**

16 fresh sardine fillets

$1/4$ cup red-wine vinegar

2 medium cloves garlic, sliced

Zest of 1 lemon

1 teaspoon sea salt

$1/2$ loaf of rustic country bread, cut into $1/2$-inch-thick slices

Oven-Roasted Eggplant (recipe follows)

1 heirloom tomato, cut into $1/4$-inch-thick slices

12 cherry tomatoes, halved

Line a Pyrex baking dish with parchment paper. Place the sardine fillets, skin side down, on the paper, making sure they're not touching one another. Pour the vinegar over the fillets and sprinkle with the garlic, lemon zest, and sea salt. Cover with another piece of parchment paper and refrigerate overnight.

The next day, preheat the broiler.

Bring the sardines to room temperature. Brush away the garlic and lemon zest.

On a broiler pan, lightly toast the bread.

To serve, put one slice of toast in the center of each of four serving plates. Top with an heirloom tomato slice and then spoon some roasted eggplant on top of one half of each slice. Lay four marinated sardine fillets, skin side up, on the other half. Garnish the plate with cherry tomatoes. (Alternatively, you may serve as an antipasti.)

Oven-Roasted Eggplant Serves 4

2 medium eggplant (about 1½ pounds)
Sea salt
¼ cup olive oil
Freshly ground black pepper

If the eggplant are young and firm, cut off the stem ends and cut the eggplant into 2-inch chunks. If they are larger, peel them and then cut into chunks.

Sprinkle the eggplant with salt and set aside in a colander for 1 hour.

Preheat the oven to 400°F.

Turn the eggplant onto a kitchen towel and blot dry. Transfer the eggplant to a baking sheet. Pour the olive oil over. Use your hands to toss. Season the eggplant with salt and pepper and bake in the oven until tender, about 40 minutes, using a spatula to turn them halfway through the cooking time.

Peekytoe Crab Salad
with Pink Grapefruit

The peekytoe crab is a small rock crab that has a little arm that's always peeking out of its shell. Not too many people knew about peekytoes until my friend Rod Mitchell (see page 28) started selling them to chefs like Daniel Boulud and Jean-Georges Vongerichten. Peekytoe meat has a subtle, sweet flavor that goes well with citrus fruits like pink grapefruit. But that flavor will disappear if you serve peekytoe crabmeat too cold, so make sure you take it out of the fridge at least an hour before you serve. If the citrus is a little too astringent for you, make this salad with apple or tomato or asparagus. You can also substitute the more expensive lump crabmeat, which is commonly found in fish markets and supermarkets. **Serves 4**

2 pink grapefruit

1 pound peekytoe or jumbo lump crabmeat, picked over (see Sources, page 237)

$1/2$ cup Sherry Vinaigrette (page 19)

$3/4$ teaspoon sea salt, plus more to finish

$1/4$ teaspoon freshly ground black pepper, plus more to finish

4 cups arugula, rinsed and spun dry

High-quality extra-virgin olive oil, for drizzling

Cut off the ends the grapefruit. Place the flat end of each grapefruit on a cutting board and cut away the peel in wide strips, from top to bottom. Hold each peeled grapefruit over a bowl and cut out the individual segments, leaving behind the membrane. Place all the segments in the bowl, along with any juice that trickles; add the crabmeat. Set aside.

Lightly dress the crabmeat and the grapefruit segments with $1/4$ cup of the Sherry Vinaigrette and some grapefruit juice (depending on how much juice the grapefruits give off and how sweet the juice is). Season with $1/2$ teaspoon of the salt and $1/4$ teaspoon black pepper. Gently toss. In another bowl, lightly dress the arugula with the remaining $1/4$ cup vinaigrette and $1/4$ teaspoon salt. Divide the dressed arugula among four bowls and top with the crabmeat salad. Drizzle each bowl with a high-quality extra-virgin olive oil, and sprinkle with crunchy sea salt and some freshly ground black pepper.

Chilled Maine Lobster
with Celery Root and Apples

One of my cooks calls this dish the Esca Waldorf Salad. In the fall I love to cook with apples and root vegetables. The Winesap apples have a spicy taste and a lovely fragrance, the celery root gives the dish a much needed savory taste, and the sweet lobster lends the whole affair some class. Don't be scared about how gnarly celery root looks in its natural state. It is, after all, a root vegetable that is not used to being seen in its birthday suit. If Winesaps are not easily found, substitute Gala, Braeburn, or Crispin apples. **Serves 4 as an appetizer**

2 live lobsters, about 1 pound each (see Ingredient Note)

2 cups apple cider

2 tablespoons plus 1 teaspoon apple cider vinegar

¼ cup extra-virgin olive oil, plus high-quality extra-virgin olive oil, for drizzling

1 teaspoon salt, plus more to finish

½ teaspoon freshly ground black pepper, plus more to finish

1 medium celery root (about 8 ounces), peeled

2 crisp apples, such as Winesap, Braeburn, Gala, or Crispin, peeled and cored

1 lemon, halved

2 cups mustard greens or other bitter green such as mizuna, or watercress

Bring a large stockpot of water to a boil. Add the live lobsters and cook for 11 minutes. Remove with tongs and set aside.

Meanwhile, in a medium saucepan, bring the apple cider to a boil over a high flame. Let it bubble away until ¾ cup remains, about 15 minutes. When cool, add the cider vinegar, the ¼ cup olive oil, 1 teaspoon salt, and ½ teaspoon pepper. Whisk to combine.

On a cutting board, use a heavy chef's knife to cut the celery root lengthwise in half. With the flat side down, cut each half into thin slices. Stack the slices, three or four at a time, and then slice into matchsticks. Toss into a mixing bowl. Cut the apples in the same way, squeezing the lemon over the apple slices to prevent browning. Dress the apple and celery root lightly with some of the cider vinaigrette, using your hands to toss (taste to adjust the salt). Toss in the bitter greens just before serving.

Twist the tails off the lobsters. Use a chef's knife to split the underside of the tails. With your hands, press the tail open and then pull the meat out of each side. Crack each claw at its widest point, remove the bottom piece of the shell, and then pull out the smaller, hinged claws. The meat will come out of the shell in one piece. Cut the meat into 2-inch chunks, leaving whole the four claws. Toss with the remaining vinaigrette.

To serve, place a small mound of the celery root salad in the center of each of four shallow bowls. Top each with one whole claw and one quarter of the lobster meat chunks. Drizzle with high-quality extra-virgin olive oil, a sprinkling of sea salt, and a few turns of freshly ground pepper.

INGREDIENT NOTE
Even though lobster is very expensive, I call it the cockroach of the sea, because that's what a lobster looks like. By the way, I'm not one of those chefs who believe that Maine lobster is necessarily better than Canadian. As long as you buy a lively hard-shell lobster, it will taste great, no matter what its provenance.

Rod Mitchell,

Fancy-Pants Fishmonger
I get a lot of good fish and shellfish from my friend Rod Mitchell, who runs his wholesale fish business, Browne Trading Company, from a dockside office in Portland, Maine. He buys tons of fish at auction, imports others, and in general knows virtually everything there is to know about fish. Rod grew up in Maine, on Peeks Island, a little island in Casco Bay, and lives there to this day. He's a marine biologist by training whose family has been in the caviar business for a hundred years. Rod first made a name for himself with chefs by selling us peekytoe crab.

He's an excellent fisherman. That makes sense to me. After all, the guy's name is Rod. He's also a very competitive man. We were fishing for bass, and Rod must have spent an hour tying this ridiculously complicated knot that he swore would yield lots of fish. But the fish were too smart for that fancy-pants knot. They kept slipping it. I told him to let me see what I could do.

I tied what I told Rod was a Long Island South Shore knot. It took me about ten seconds. As soon as I put my line in the water, I caught a big bass, a twenty-pounder, then another, and finally a third, all in fifteen minutes. Rod was getting madder and madder. I stopped laughing long enough to tell him that I would teach him the legendary South Shore knot. He didn't seem that interested to learn.

Roasted Porcini
with Lamb's Lettuce and Aged Goat Cheese

To me, porcini mushrooms are very Italian, though we are now cultivating them in America. I prefer the more concentrated and more expansive Italian porcini, and roasting them really intensifies their flavor. When buying porcini, make sure they are dry, and before cooking them cut one in half to make sure there are no worms. The best and easiest way to clean mushrooms is to gently rub them with a damp paper towel. When porcinis are not in season, substitute cremini or regular button mushrooms. Lamb's lettuce, also known as mâche, has delicate leaves, so in winter, use baby spinach or arugula in this dish. **Serves 4**

3 tablespoons olive oil, plus more if necessary

**1 pound fresh porcini mushrooms,
    stems cut in half, tops left whole**

1 lemon, halved

Sea salt

Freshly ground black pepper

4 cups mâche, or baby spinach or arugula

**Parmigiano-Reggiano Vinaigrette
    (recipe follows)**

**6 ounces aged goat cheese
    (I prefer Coach Farm)**

Heat the olive oil in a large sauté pan over a medium-high flame. When the oil is hot but not smoking, add the porcini stems. Don't move the pan for 2 minutes, until the stems take on some color. Then turn the stems and brown them on all sides, about 7 minutes total. Transfer the stems to a bowl and squeeze half a lemon over them, along with some salt and pepper. Replenish the oil in the pan if necessary and repeat with the mushroom caps, using the other lemon half when the caps are done.

When the porcini have all been sautéed, dress them lightly (use about 3 to 4 tablespoons) with the Parmigiano-Reggiano Vinaigrette. Use your hands to toss.

In another bowl, lightly dress the mâche with the remaining vinaigrette, tossing to coat thoroughly.

To serve the salad, make beds of dressed greens on four serving plates. Top each with an equal mound of porcini, and then crumble the aged goat cheese over. Finish with some sea salt and freshly ground black pepper.

Parmigiano-Reggiano Vinaigrette Makes ¾ cup

¼ cup fresh lemon juice (about 2 lemons)

¼ cup finely grated Parmigiano-Reggiano

½ cup extra-virgin olive oil

¼ teaspoon sea salt

½ teaspoon freshly ground black pepper

In a small bowl, whisk the lemon juice and Parmesan into the olive oil, and season with the salt and pepper

Corn Salad
with Walnuts and Goat Cheese

This is the single most requested item on the Esca menu in the summer and early fall, when fresh corn is at its peak in the Northeast. I roast the corn to intensify its sweetness and give it an understated smoky flavor. When you're toasting the walnuts, watch them carefully—do not walk away from the pan, even for a moment, as they go from toasted to burned in seconds. **Serves 4**

6 ears corn, husked (see Ingredient Notes)

¼ cup walnuts

½ cup Rosemary Oil (recipe follows)

½ cup Braised Mushrooms (page 93), preferably chanterelle

3 tablespoons unsalted butter

4 ounces dry aged goat cheese finely grated using the small holes of a box grater (see Ingredient Notes)

Sea salt

Freshly ground black pepper

4 cups arugula, rinsed and spun-dry

Preheat the oven to 300°F.

Prepare a charcoal fire. Grill the corn over the fire until lightly charred, about 3 minutes. Cut off the narrow end of the cob. Hold the ear with one hand, the flat end resting on a cutting board, and cut the kernels from the cob. Place the kernels in a bowl. Repeat with each ear of corn. Set the corn kernels aside.

Place the walnuts on a baking tray and toast in the oven for 3 minutes, or until they begin to give off an aroma. Remove from the oven and set aside.

In a large sauté pan, heat 2 tablespoons of the Rosemary Oil. Slightly crush the toasted walnuts in your hand and add to the pan along with the Braised Mushrooms. Sauté for 1 minute. Add the corn kernels, stir to combine, and sauté for 3 minutes, until the corn is hot. Add the butter and 2 tablespoons of the grated goat cheese. Season with salt and pepper.

Place the arugula leaves in a mixing bowl. Dress them with most of the Rosemary Oil and season with salt and pepper. To serve, spoon the corn mixture into the center of four serving plates and sprinkle with half the remaining goat cheese. Top with the arugula and the rest of the goat cheese. Drizzle each plate with some of the remaining Rosemary Oil.

continued

Many people think white corn varieties are sweeter than their yellow counterparts. Not so. In fact, the most important thing to know about buying corn is when it was picked. Corn's natural sugar turns to starch the longer it's been off the stalk.

It's worth it to use an artisanal domestic goat cheese like Coach Farm here. It has a cleaner taste and creamier texture.

Rosemary Oil Makes ½ cup

½ cup olive oil
2 sprigs rosemary

Place the olive oil in a small saucepan and add the rosemary. Heat over a low flame until the oil is warm, but not hot. Reserve until the oil is cool. Strain and discard the rosemary sprigs.

Grilled Tomatoes with Bread Crumbs and Anchovies

I first had this dish at Tatou, a legendary restaurant that a chef friend recommended in the south of France in the town of Juan-les-Pins. It's one of only five dishes on the menu there. It is delicious and so easy to make: just make sure you're using sweet vine-ripened tomatoes and the best bread crumbs you can find. This dish works well with either fresh or high-quality salted anchovies. **Serves 4**

**2 pounds fresh Brandywine
    or canned San Marzano tomatoes**

Sea salt

1 cup extra-virgin olive oil

¼ cup fresh basil leaves

2 cups Italian-Style Bread Crumbs (page 233)

**18 marinated white anchovies
    (about 1 pound; sold by your fishmonger)**

Freshly ground black pepper

Slice the tomatoes lengthwise into ¼-inch slices and place on a cooling rack set over a baking tray. Lightly salt and let stand for a half hour, to reduce their water content. Gently press with paper towels.

Preheat the broiler.

In an oval, enameled cast-iron gratin dish, make a single layer of one-third of the tomato slices. Drizzle with some extra-virgin olive oil and spread about 8 basil leaves over them. Sprinkle with a dusting of bread crumbs and spread about six anchovies on top of that, followed by several grinds of black pepper. Repeat to form three layers, finishing with a top layer of bread crumbs, a generous drizzle of olive oil, and some black pepper.

Broil until the top is golden brown and the gratin is heated through, about 7 minutes. Serve immediately.

Zucchini Blossoms Stuffed with
Anchovies &
Mozzarella

Everywhere I went in Naples with the legendary cook Rita de Rosa, we were confronted by zucchini blossoms, which take very well to deep-frying as long as your batter is not too heavy. Use fresh anchovies if you can find them; if not, spend the money to get one of the good brands of tinned anchovies, which are more saline and less fishy. And try to find fresh cow's milk mozzarella or, better yet, splurge for the mozzarella di bufala imported from Italy (see Sources, page 237). **Serves 4**

1½ pounds fresh mozzarella,
    cut into ½-inch dice

16 fresh anchovies, roughly chopped

16 zucchini blossoms

3 large eggs

2 cups all-purpose flour

1 teaspoon sea salt

1 teaspoon freshly ground black pepper

Olive oil

2 bunches arugula (about 2 cups),
    rinsed and spun-dry

¼ cup Sherry Vinaigrette (page 19)

In a mixing bowl, combine the mozzarella with the anchovies. Gently spoon about 2 to 3 tablespoons of the mixture into each zucchini blossom, but be careful not to overfill, the flower should not look "stuffed" and the petals should be able to close over the filling.

In one shallow bowl, lightly beat the eggs; in another, combine the flour with the salt and pepper. Dust the blossoms with the seasoned flour, then dip each in the beaten eggs, and then give the flowers another light dredging in flour.

Heat 2 inches of olive oil over a medium-high flame until hot but not smoking. Use a spatula to transfer the stuffed blossoms to the pan and cook, in batches if necessary, until the flowers are golden brown all around, 6 to 8 minutes total; they should be crispy with a molten warm center. Transfer to a paper-towel-lined plate.

Toss the arugula with the vinaigrette. Serve the zucchini blossoms, four per plate, over the lightly dressed greens.

INGREDIENT NOTE

Buy zucchini blossoms at a farmer's market or specialty store. Keep them out of the heat, and try to purchase them as close as possible to the time you'll be cooking them.

Inguazato

This is a great one-pot dish that I've eaten many times in Rome. I serve this when my in-laws are coming over, because they're a tough crowd, and they know their Italian food. Monkfish has a lobsterlike texture and a mild flavor. The couscous adds some body and stretches it a little farther. **Serves 4**

3 tablespoons extra-virgin olive oil

2 cloves garlic, thinly sliced

**2 mild dried red chiles
(such as Italian finger hots)**

**One 28-ounce can cherry tomatoes and
their juice (see Sources, page 237)
or canned plum tomatoes**

12 large Sicilian olives, cracked

1 cup couscous

Four 6-ounce monkfish tails

Heat the olive oil in a large, enameled sauté pan over a medium flame until hot but not smoking. Add the garlic and the chiles and cook until the garlic is translucent, 3 to 4 minutes. Add the cherry tomatoes, with their juice, and the olives and bring to a simmer over a medium flame. Cook until the cherry tomatoes begin to break down, about 10 minutes.

Stir the couscous into the simmering tomatoes, then rest the monkfish tails on top of the simmering ingredients. Cook, covered, for 6 minutes, turn the tails over, and continue cooking for 6 more minutes.

Bring the enameled pan to the table, place on a trivet, and serve family-style.

Zuppe di Pesce Amalfitano

When you're making a fish soup, the broth is everything. There's always good fish soup on the Amalfi Coast, where each town has a slightly different version. This is my own Hell's Kitchen version, intensely flavorful and complex—this is not *zuppa* for the faint of heart. I use the sweeter, imported canned tomatoes with the DOC label on them. (In 1955 Italy enacted DOC laws to safeguard the names, characteristics, and origins of certain Italian foods.) Don't be afraid to use oilier fish in your *zuppe*, like mackerel and monkfish, which lend tons of flavor. If you use shrimp, leave them in the shell or else they'll dry out. The anise liqueur adds an interesting licorice flavor. Prepare the broth the day before to make it easier on yourself, and to allow the broth's flavor to intensify. **Serves 4**

¼ cup extra-virgin olive oil, plus high-quality extra-virgin olive oil, for drizzling

5 cloves garlic

1 fennel bulb, coarsely chopped

1 small leek, washed well and coarsely chopped

1 stalk celery, coarsely chopped

Sea salt

Freshly ground black pepper

4 fresh Roma or canned San Marzano tomatoes, halved

3 cups canned San Marzano tomatoes and their juice

1 cup white wine

1 cup Ricard (or other anise liqueur)

2 sprigs parsley

2 sprigs thyme

1 bay leaf

1 teaspoon whole black peppercorns

2 pounds fish bones, cleaned

1 pound assorted fresh fish fillets (cod, bass, flounder, salmon, grouper), cut into 2-inch pieces

Chopped parsley, for garnish

Heat the ¼ cup olive oil in a large stockpot or Dutch oven. Add the garlic, fennel, leek, and celery. Cook, stirring occasionally, until the vegetables are translucent, 7 to 10 minutes. Season with 1 teaspoon salt and ¼ teaspoon black pepper. Add the fresh tomatoes and continue cooking until they begin to break down, about 10 minutes.

Add the canned tomatoes, wine, Ricard, parsley, thyme, bay leaf, and peppercorns. Bring to a boil over a high flame, then reduce the heat to a simmer. Cook

continued

until the tomatoes have broken down substantially, 15 to 20 minutes, stirring frequently throughout. Add the fish bones and enough water so that the bones are covered. Stir while the pot simmers for 20 minutes. Strain the liquid through a fine-mesh sieve. Let cool, then refrigerate for up to 2 days.

Before using, skim the surface of any impurities that rise to the top.

Reheat the *zuppa* in a stockpot over a medium flame until gently simmering. Season with salt and pepper to taste. Add the fish pieces and cook for about 6 minutes; the fish should be well cooked and flaky. Ladle the soup into serving bowls. Add the chopped parsley just before serving, and drizzle with a high-quality extra-virgin olive oil.

Brodetto

I vividly remember the first time I ate brodetto in a great restaurant in Amalfi called Da Zaccaria—I can still smell the garlic and the perfume of the shellfish mixture cooked in a tomatoless broth with hot red pepper and basil. Don't put all the shellfish in the pan at once; staggering their entrance preserves more of their individual flavors. **Serves 4**

8 ounces Clam Stock (page 75)

1 cup gigante beans
    (with about ¼ cup of their cooking liquid)

3 to 4 dried arbol chiles

4 cloves garlic, crushed

1 tablespoon extra-virgin olive oil

5 pounds mixed shellfish
    (mahogany, Manila, or razor clams;
    mussels; Taylor Bay scallops)

½ cup flat-leaf parsley leaves

½ cup fresh basil leaves

Sea salt

Freshly ground black pepper

In a large heavy-bottomed pot with a tight-fitting lid, combine the Clam Stock with the beans and their cooking liquid, the chiles, garlic, and olive oil. Bring to a boil.

Add the clams, cover, and cook until they open, 4 to 6 minutes. Discard any shells that haven't opened. Add the mussels and scallops, cover, and cook for 3 to 4 minutes more, until the shells open. Again, discard any that haven't. Add the parsley and basil, stir to combine, and season with salt and pepper. Serve immediately.

Crudo

I've been eating crudo since I was a kid. Back then it didn't have a name. I'd go out fishing with my dad, and once all the Skittles and Mountain Dew were consumed, and we'd had some luck fishing, my dad would take a knife, gut and clean the fish right there on the boat. He'd cut some pristine, ultra-thin slices, sprinkle some lemon juice and Morton's salt on it, and that, my friends, would be that. It was a delicious if crude form of what my partner Joe Bastianich would later name crudo.

I never thought much about what we had eaten on the boat as I got older. Every once in a while, when I'd be out fishing with my pal Artie Hoenig, we'd do what my dad did, and end up with a great impromptu on-board lunch. It always struck me that as much as I loved sushi, the combination of perfectly fresh raw fish, good olive oil, sea salt, and some kind of citrus juice took raw fish preparation to even greater heights. The soy sauce can sometimes drown out the complex taste of the fish, while fresh herbs and olive oil tend to expand our flavor palettes.

But I never thought about serving crudo at a restaurant until my partners Joe Bastianich, Mario Batali, and I took a trip to Trieste and Istria in 2000 for some good old-fashioned chef R&D (research and development), eating and drinking pretty much continually 16 hours a day, in search of inspiration for Esca, the new seafood restaurant we were opening.

Joe seemed to know every fisherman, chef, and restaurateur in each town we visited. These were his people, after all. In the sixties, his parents, Felix and Lidia, had escaped an Istrian detention camp amid a hail of bullets to come to America under the auspices of a Catholic youth organization. To stay in touch with their roots, the entire Bastianich clan often returned to Istria.

We would pull into tiny villages on the Istrian coast and be warmly welcomed by a long-lost Bastianich friend or relative. We spent days and nights eating in tiny trattorias and tavernas that had a small bar where the locals would drink and chain-smoke, with hooks on the outside wall where fishermen would leave their fresh catch. The chef-owner would slice the fish super-thin and serve it with some combination of olive oil, herbs, citrus juice—lemon, lime or clementine. I was reminded of what we had done on Artie's boat for all these years, but these folks were taking the concept to a whole new level. We were all blown away.

One beautiful evening we were busily consuming lots of raw fish and the Bastianichs' own wine. Mario, Joe, and I were in seafood heaven. Joe, ever the entrepreneur, announced, "See this raw fish. Let's call it *pesce crudo,* or maybe just crudo. We're going to serve crudo at Esca. How could we not? If we are going to be a great Italian seafood restaurant, crudo can set us apart."

When we got home and developed our menu in the Esca kitchen, I started creating crudo combinations on the fly: Black Sea Bass with Pine Nuts, Albacore with Caperberries, Nantucket Bay Scallops with Lemon and Chervil (all of which you will find on the pages that follow). I was using the basic cooking and food knowledge I had acquired over the years and applying it to raw fish: combining salty and sweet, sweet and sour, crunchy and tender, oil and citrus. I felt as if we were on to something. I didn't know if customers would like it, but Mario, Joe, and I sure did.

One day Mario and Joe came into the Esca kitchen as I was preparing some striped bass with pine nuts, Meyer lemon juice, and Sicilian sea salt. Mario took a piece, closed his eyes, swallowed, and immediately a huge grin came across his face. "You did it, dude. This rocks. You totally reinvented the wheel. We are going to kick some serious ass with this crudo." Joe, ever the cool, calm, and collected businessman, was just as enthusiastic in his own way. "You totally get crudo, Dave. I knew you would. You watch. We're gonna sell a ton of crudo at Esca. It's what's going to define the restaurant."

PREPARATION NOTE

A lot of people tell me that they would be afraid to make crudo at home. They shouldn't be. Obviously it's imperative to use very fresh fish. If you're not a fisher person yourself, you need to develop a relationship with a local fishmonger. A wise man once told me about buying seafood: "You don't buy the fish. You buy the man." It's true. An honest fishmonger will always steer you to the freshest fish he or she's got, especially if the individual knows that you're serving it raw. Once your fishmonger selects your fish for you, ask him or her to cut it into crudo-size slices.

Slicing raw fish is a practiced skill. Cut the fish while it's cold, but serve it just cooler than room temperature. Use a heavy, sharp knife with a straight (not serrated) blade. The fish can be sliced hours in advance, and refrigerated in a Pyrex or glass dish, covered with parchment paper, and then covered with plastic wrap. That will remove the final impediment to making restaurant-quality crudo at home.

If you don't have access to a good fish market in your town, there are a number of fish purveyors across the country who will send you impeccably fresh fish overnight. You'll pay through the nose for the overnight shipping, but you'll be assured of getting the quality of fish you need. I have listed these purveyors in the back of the book (see Sources, page 237).

Albacore Crudo with Caperberries

Albacore tuna is the same species used in common canned tuna like Bumble Bee and Chicken of the Sea. It's fished in local waters on the East Coast in the summer, so that's when I serve it at the restaurant. It's a fatty fish, and that fat gives albacore a ton of flavor. I like to serve it as crudo with caperberries, which add just the right touch of acidity. **Serves 6**

3 lemons, halved
1 pound albacore fillet
Fine sea salt

Freshly ground black pepper
High-quality extra-virgin olive oil, for drizzling
16 Sicilian caperberries

Put a small puddle of lemon juice—about 1 tablespoon each—in the center of six small serving plates then drizzle the lemon juice around the sides of the plates. The lemon juice is put under the fish so that it will not discolor it.

Slice the albacore in the same way that the sea bass fillets are on page 65. Arrange the slices on the serving plates atop the puddles of lemon juice.

Sprinkle a few crunchy grains of sea salt on each slice of fish. Follow with a light grinding of black pepper on each piece and then a light drizzle of high-quality olive oil over the top. Add 4 caperberries to each plate and serve immediately.

Razor Clam Crudo

These long, thin clams, which Chinese chefs love, can get really rubbery when you cook them, so using them in a crudo preparation will eliminate a lot of the guesswork from working with them. Putting the clams back in the shells makes for a dramatic presentation. The live clams should react when you touch the shells by springing closed. Discard those that don't. **Serves 4**

1/4 cup plus 1 teaspoon sea salt

2 pounds razor clams

1 sprig mint, leaves picked over, rolled, and thinly sliced

2 scallions, thinly sliced on the diagonal

1 mild red chile (such as Italian finger hot), seeds discarded, minced

1 tablespoon fresh lemon juice

1 tablespoon fresh lime juice

3 tablespoons extra-virgin olive oil

Pinch of freshly ground black pepper

Prepare a large bowl of ice water with about 1/4 cup of salt in it. Shuck the clams and reserve their juice in a jar or container. Cut the belly on the bias, then peel and discard the membrane. (You can ask your fishmonger to do this for you, but be sure to keep the shells and the juice.) Place the razor clams in the ice water for about 10 minutes; this draws the sand from them. Meanwhile, rinse the shells to serve the crudo in.

Use a slotted spoon to remove the razor clams from the ice water. Place them in a glass mixing bowl along with 1 tablespoon of the clam juice (the sand will have settled to the bottom of the container, so draw the tablespoon from the top). Add the mint, scallions, chile, lemon juice, lime juice, olive oil, the remaining 1 teaspoon salt, and the pepper. Mix well to thoroughly combine. Spoon the crudo onto the clam shells and serve on a platter right away.

"**BLUEFISH** is the **MEANEST, NASTIEST** fish on the water—they eat anything in their way, **ANYTHING.**"

Bluefish Tartare

There are a lot of bluefish haters out there, and I designed this dish to convert them. The key to falling in love with bluefish is using only the small ones, known as snapper blues, which have a much cleaner, less fishy taste; their flesh is also much less oily. The preserved lemon adds the zip to this dish. If you can't find preserved lemon and don't want to go to the trouble of making it, use lemon zest instead; but do not use lemon juice, which would cook the fish ceviche-style. This is one dish that depends on your relationship with your fishmonger. Tell that person what you're planning to make, and he or she should advise you whether the bluefish on hand is right for the dish. **Serves 4**

One 2-pound bluefish, scaled, cleaned, filleted, skinned, and blood line removed

1 teaspoon Dijon mustard

1 teaspoon chopped preserved lemon or lemon zest

1 teaspoon chopped chives

1 teaspoon coarse sea salt

Freshly ground black pepper

High-quality extra-virgin olive oil, for drizzling

Coarsely chop the fish. In a large bowl, gently combine the fish with the mustard, preserved lemon, and chives.

Divide among four plates. Season each serving with sea salt and freshly ground black pepper, then drizzle with the extra-virgin olive oil. Serve immediately.

Above: Fluke. **Right:** Fluke with Sea Beans and Radishes (page 56).

Fluke with Sea Beans and Radishes

Fluke is fished year-round where I live, even though it is also known as summer flounder. Although it's a common, relatively inexpensive fish, fluke actually makes the most surprisingly tender, cleanly flavored, and firm-fleshed crudo. Sea beans are those weird green things you see right off the shore at the beach. They add great crunch and saltiness to the dish. If you can't find sea beans, use additional thinly cut radish slices instead. The radishes add just the right touch of acidity. **Serves 4**

4 ounces sea beans
4 ounces radishes, cut into matchsticks
Coarse sea salt

Juice of ½ lime
One 8-ounce fluke fillet
High-quality extra-virgin olive oil, for drizzling

In a small mixing bowl, combine the sea beans, radishes, a pinch of sea salt, and a squeeze of lime juice.

Using a knife with a thin sharp blade, begin cutting the fluke into thin slices on the diagonal. Transfer the slices to four serving plates as they are cut, forming a fan pattern, about four slices per plate.

Place a small mound of the sea bean salad on top of the fanned fluke in the center of each plate. Drizzle each serving with olive oil and a sprinkling of sea salt. Serve immediately.

Photograph on page 55

Two-Minute Cherrystone Clam Ceviche

Ceviche is a Latino or South American preparation in which the fish flesh is essentially "cooked" by the acidity of whatever citrus juice it's quickly marinated in. The crucial mistake most people make with ceviche is letting the fish or shellfish marinate too long, and the fish becomes tough. So I figure if I name the dish two-minute ceviche, people will get the idea. Rinse the shells of the clams and serve the ceviche right in them. Scallops or shrimp also would work just as well. **Serves 4**

Juice of 2 lemons (about ¼ cup)

Juice of 5 limes (about ¼ cup)

1 dozen cherrystone clams, shucked

½ cup diced yellow (or red) watermelon

½ large cucumber, peeled, seeded, and finely diced (about ½ cup)

3 scallions, cut paper-thin on the bias

1 jalepeño, seeds removed, finely diced (about 2 teaspoons)

2 tablespoons extra-virgin olive oil, plus high-quality extra-virgin olive oil, for drizzling

Course sea salt

Combine the lemon and lime juices in a glass mixing bowl. Add the clams and let sit for 2 minutes. Pour the citrus juices out while keeping the fish in the bowl with a large strainer or slotted spoon. Add the watermelon, cucumber, scallions, jalepeño, and the 2 tablespoons olive oil. Toss gently to combine.

Serve the ceviche in the rinsed shells or in chilled individual serving bowls. Drizzle each serving and shells with extra-virgin olive oil and season with coarse sea salt. Serve immediately.

Weakfish
with Chives

Weakfish, also known as sea trout, has a nice creamy, buttery, meaty flavor. Think of this dish as the crudo equivalent of cream cheese with chives. In fact, if you put a couple of pieces of this crudo on a bagel, it would taste really great. **Serves 4**

2 weakfish fillets (about 6 ounces each)
Juice of ½ lemon
3 chives, sliced very thin

Coarse sea salt
Freshly ground black pepper
High-quality extra-virgin olive oil, for drizzling

Cut each weakfish fillet into four strips from nose to tail, first in half along where the spine would be, then the belly and top halves. Cut away the tip ends so that the strips are fairly rectangular, and of equal thickness. Then cut each rectangle into crudo slices about 2 inches wide and ¼ inch thick. Cut the strips on the bias using a very sharp straight blade. Move your fingers back, slice by slice, making a clean, sure cut.

To serve, arrange an equal number of slices of fish on each of four serving plates. You will have between 4 and 6 slices per person. Top each slice with just a drop of lemon juice, a light sprinkling of chives, a light sprinkling of sea salt and pepper, and a light drizzle of olive oil. Serve immediately.

Ruby Red Shrimp Crudo

I know you're not going to believe this, but if you close your eyes while you're eating this dish, you'll swear you're eating peanut butter. That's because this small, fatty shrimp, native to the Gulf of Maine, has an incredibly rich flavor. And like peanut butter, the fat sticks to the roof of your mouth. Like most crudo preparations, this one depends on using the right components. Use a fruity, Sicilian olive oil (see Sources, page 237), sea salt, and the sweetest lemons you can find. This is one dish that doesn't allow for substitutes. Do not try to make this crudo with conventional Gulf shrimp. **Serves 4**

½ pound ruby red shrimp, peeled and deveined

Juice of ½ lemon

4 tablespoons high-quality extra-virgin olive oil, preferably Sicilian

Pinch of fine sea salt

Freshly ground black pepper

In a bowl, combine the shrimp, lemon juice, olive oil, salt, and pepper. Mix well. Serve immediately.

Wild Striped Bass with Pumpkin Seeds

This crudo preparation is inspired by fall. Wild striped bass is a bigger, meatier, slightly gamier fish than black sea bass, and it seems to have become a staple on restaurant menus all over the country. Farm-raised striped bass is a totally different fish, and should not be used here. The wild variety should have opaque flesh if it's reasonably fresh. Toast the pumpkin seeds slow and long, and you'll find they develop a terrific nuttiness. **Serves 4**

¼ cup shelled pumpkin seeds
½ teaspoon fine sea salt, plus more to finish
Pinch of cayenne pepper
1 pound wild striped bass fillets

Juice of ½ lemon
High-quality extra-virgin olive oil, for drizzling
Freshly ground black pepper to finish

Preheat the oven to 250°F.

Spread the pumpkin seeds on a small baking sheet. Sprinkle with the ½ teaspoon salt and a pinch of cayenne pepper, and toss. Bake in the oven, shaking the pan occasionally, until the seeds are dry and crunchy, about 2 hours. Let cool before using.

Cut each fillet into four strips from nose to tail, first in half along where the spine would be, then the belly and top halves. Cut away the tip ends so that the strips are fairly rectangular, and of equal thickness. Then cut each rectangle into crudo slices about 2 inches wide and ¼ inch thick. Cut the strips on the bias using a very sharp straight blade. Move your fingers back, slice by slice, making a clean, sure cut.

Arrange the slices of fish in a pinwheel shape on four serving plates (about four slices per serving). Top each slice with just a drop of lemon juice, a light sprinkling of sea salt, a drizzle of olive oil, and two toasted pumpkin seeds. Finish with a dusting of freshly ground black pepper. Serve immediately.

Nantucket Bay Scallops with Lemon and Chervil

When I'm starting with something as good as Nantucket Bay scallops (which are as good as good gets), I feel it's my job as a cook to stay out of the way and let the scallops speak for themselves. In other words, don't mess with perfection. Here, the little bit of lemon adds a touch of acidity to a naturally rich foodstuff, and the chervil lends some grassy neutrality that doesn't overpower or detract from the scallops. **Serves 4**

½ **pound Nantucket Bay scallops (about 25 to 30), well chilled**

Juice of ½ lemon

¼ **cup extra-virgin olive oil**

Coarse sea salt

Freshly ground black pepper

2 sprigs chervil, leaves only

In a mixing bowl, combine the scallops, lemon juice, and olive oil. Toss gently to combine. Spoon onto four serving plates and dress each with a light sprinkling of sea salt, black pepper, and a few chervil leaves. Serve immediately.

Scallops

- **Diver scallops** are superior-quality sea scallops caught by scuba divers in Maine from December 1 to April 15. My diver scallop guy, Alf, is a one-man business. One time I bought 26 pounds from him at $14.50 a pound. That's one day's work for him. It's tough work. He dives for an hour or two, then he comes up for an hour to avoid hypothermia. Diver scallops are expensive, but they are worth it. They're sweet and nutty and tender if you don't overcook them. Diver scallops have firmer flesh than dredged sea scallops (see below), and they're bigger and pinker. Some diver scallops have a faint orange-yellow tinge. That just means they're spawning. Most people won't buy them when they're that color, but they should, because they taste great.

- **Conventionally harvested sea scallops** are dredged, meaning they are swept up by big rakes that trail from boats. These boats often go out for weeks at a time, and as a result those scallops are treated with sodium phosphate, to preserve them. Avoid those scallops like the plague, because that chemical leaches their flavor. Always look for what are called dry scallops, which are untreated.

- **Bay scallops** are caught in Nantucket Bay and in Peconic Bay, off the east end of Long Island. They're smaller than sea scallops, but they're absolutely wonderful, sweet as cotton candy, and almost as soft. Bay scallops have a three-year life span. In their first year of life they're too small to harvest. In their second year they are harvested. In their third year, if they haven't been harvested, they spawn and then die. Brown tide has made bay scallops pretty scarce the last couple of years, and from year to year it's difficult to predict how many of them are going to be harvested.

- **Scallops in the shell** can sometimes be found in their fan-shaped shells at fancy fish markets. I use them in crudo preparations, for steaming, and for pasta dishes that I serve with seafood in the shell.

Black Sea Bass with Pine Nuts

People are always surprised at how good this dish is, and I don't know why. Black sea bass has a lovely sweet taste—it's one of the best-tasting, readily available East Coast fish— and it's fatty enough to stand up to the pine nuts. Black sea bass is not cheap, but it's well worth the money. When buying, make sure the flesh has a pinkish tinge; if it's too white, black sea bass can be a little milky tasting. I send it back to my fishmonger if it's too white, and you should, too. **Serves 4**

2 tablespoons pine nuts
Two 6-ounce black sea bass fillets
Juice of ½ lemon

Coarse sea salt
Freshly ground black pepper
High-quality extra-virgin olive oil, for drizzling

Preheat the oven to 300°F. Spread the pine nuts on a baking sheet and toast for 3 minutes. Let cool.

Cut each fillet into four strips from nose to tail, first in half along where the spine would be, then the belly and top halves. Cut away the tip ends so that the strips are fairly rectangular, and of equal thickness. Then cut each rectangle into crudo slices about 2 inches wide and ¼-inch thick. Cut the strips on the bias using a very sharp straight blade. Move your fingers back, slice by slice, making a clean, sure cut. There should be at least 16 slices, though the size and shape of the fillets may allow for more or less.

To serve, arrange four slices of the fish on each of four serving plates. Top each slice with just a drop of lemon juice, a light sprinkling of sea salt and pepper, a light drizzle of olive oil, and a few pine nuts. Serve immediately.

Striped Bass Fishing Adventure with Ed Levine

I decided that if Ed was going to write this book, he had to go fishing with me at least once. One gorgeous, surprisingly mild late-fall day, Ed took the 10:30 A.M. train from Manhattan's Penn Station out to my house in Long Beach. Of course you would have never known it was such a warm day from looking at how Ed was dressed. He had on a ski parka, flannel-lined pants covered by cross-country ski pants, and knee-high black rubber boots. He was ready for anything except the gorgeous day he was being confronted with.

We were going out on my friend Mike's boat with my friend Jim in search of striped bass. Mike is a commercial fisherman and fish wholesaler. He's crazy, but he's also some kind of tenacious. He will not come home empty-handed from a fishing excursion. I had told him not to get crazy with Ed in the boat, to get him back in time to make the 6:48 train to New York. Mike had acknowledged this request with a weird half-smile; he doesn't like time constraints placed on his fishing excursions. Jim has a day job as a petrochemical ship inspector and a contracting business on the side, but somehow manages to find time to fish almost every day. His explanation for this: "I'm supposed to be on a ship, and I am."

To call Mike's boat a ship is a bit of a stretch. It's your basic 17-foot boat. There's no cockpit, no windshield; just a steering wheel, throttle, and fish finder. But as far as I'm concerned, that's all you need. Usually, if I go out fishing with Mike, I bring a big lunch, because you could be out for a long time. But since Mike had promised me he wouldn't torture Ed with one of his endless fishing days, I didn't bring anything at all. Mike had brought a half-case of Diet Sierra Mist, and Jim had bought a package of Skittles—ahh, the breakfast of fishing champions.

We had a burlap bag of skipper clams to use as bait, but the fish were utterly uninterested in those. After an hour without a nibble, Mike and Jim were getting really agitated. Neither of them is a proponent of the "Isn't it lovely to be out on a boat," Zen school of fishing. To no one in particular, Mike proclaimed, "I *hate* fishing, but I *love* catching."

Mike decided that live bait was the answer to our problems. He gunned the boat to a blackfish spot located by his fish finder. In short order we caught ten little 1-pound blackfish, perfect appetizers for a striped bass in search of lunch. Mike, Jim, and I each put a live blackfish on our hooks. Two minutes later, Jim had a bite. His feet planted firmly on the floor, knees slightly bent, Jim started furiously trying to reel it in. In a short time, Jim pulled a 20-pound striper into the boat and disengaged the hook from the fish's mouth. The fish's blood and guts were all over the boat, and I sensed that Ed had never seen anything like this.

New York State laws allow each recreational fisherman to catch one striped bass apiece. So we had three more to catch. A few minutes later Mike's line went taut. A minute or so later he caught an even bigger striped bass. The mood in the boat had changed. We were all feeling good waiting for the next bite. Well, maybe not quite everyone. Ed was looking a little green at the gills.

I caught the next fish, a similar-sized striper, and all that was left to do was catch one more. I told Ed, "The next one is yours, so get ready." Ed was taking pictures of the sunset, so I can't say he looked ready. A few minutes went by, and then I had another bite. I shoved the rod into Ed's hands, and told him now was the time. Ed looked panic-stricken. He started to reel the fish in. About two minutes later (Ed told me afterward it felt like an hour) Ed's striped bass appeared on the side of the boat out of the water. By the time we put Ed's fish on ice, his clothes were covered with fish blood and guts. He wasn't ready for the untidiness that comes with catching fish. I think it's safe to say that Ed looked more bewildered than triumphant.

Miraculously, when we took the striped bass off the hook, the blackfish was still alive. Our bait was going to live to see another day, or perhaps I should say sunset, and so was Ed. He caught the 6:48 train home, but his life had changed forever in that last hour on the boat. He had caught his first fish.

Pasta

When most cooks and eaters think about seafood and pasta, they think about linguine with clam sauce. But at my house and at my restaurant, we combine pasta and seafood in really cool ways that go far beyond clam sauce. Some I learned on trips to Italy with friends and family. Others I learned from sitting around the table talking to colleagues, like my partners, Molto and Joe and Lidia Bastianich. And some combinations just come to me as a by-product of what pastas I have on hand and what seafood comes into the restaurant that day. If somebody calls me with some beautiful squid, I create a pasta special with squid and spicy tomato sauce. Nothing earth-shatteringly original there, just commonsense cooking that people gravitate to naturally.

In general, I have developed a few rules to cook by when it comes to combining pasta with fish and shellfish:

- The shape dictates the dish. Certain shapes go with certain kinds of sauces or ingredients. I know it's a cliché, but linguine does go with clams. But it also goes with *bottarga,* and that is not something you see often. Tagliatelle is a delicate Emilian pasta made with eggs and flour, and it goes beautifully with delicately flavored scallops or crabmeat or lobster. You wouldn't put rigatoni with garlic and oil. It just wouldn't work. Rigatoni needs something that's going to coat the pasta well and get inside of it.

- The general practice, or the one that was drummed into me by traditionally minded Italian cooks, is no cheese with fish. But I find that milder cheeses like ricotta, mozzarella, or mild feta can work very well in certain pasta preparations. I personally don't use Parmigiano-Reggiano or Pecorino Romano in seafood and pasta preparations, as I think they just overwhelm anything they touch. When people ask for grated cheese for their pasta at Esca, our servers offer toasted seasoned bread crumbs instead.

- After I've cooked my pasta about 90 percent of the way through in boiling water, I invariably finish it in a sauté pan with a little bit of the pasta water and the sauce. It adds a little coating, a little starch to the dish.

- The way you sauce a pasta is very important. Molto taught me sparseness in terms of saucing. He told me that you sauce a pasta the way you dress a salad. You don't overdress a salad, and you don't drown your pasta in sauce. Because pasta dishes are by definition more about the pasta than anything else. The sauce is a condiment—it's like the ketchup on a hamburger.

- I always serve clams, mussels, and lobster in the shell with pasta. The shell seals in the flavor. I know it can sometimes seem like a lot of unnecessary work to wrestle with shells, but in the end it's all about maximizing flavor and deliciousness. And for that result, shells are the way to go.

- The choice of dried versus fresh pasta with seafood depends on how I'm using the seafood. If I'm using fresh pasta, I'll take the shrimp out of the shell, because of the way fresh pasta lays on the plate. Conversely, with dried pasta, I'll leave the shell on the shrimp, because the shell adds flavor and texture to the sauce. We use mostly fresh pastas made in-house at the restaurant, and I give you a couple of those recipes here. But if you have a fresh pasta shop near your house, buy theirs. Or just use a good dried pasta like Latini, Martelli, or DeCecco. Those brands have a coarser texture that holds the sauce better.

- When you're cooking seafood to go with pasta, you want to retain the liquor, the liquid that's in the shell, because that's where a lot of the flavor is. That liquor is the key to the success of many pasta-seafood combinations. You wouldn't throw out the pan juices when you cook a steak, would you? Of course not.

- With some of my pasta dishes, like Tagliatelle with Nantucket Bay Scallops (opposite), I just warm the scallops, because if you really cooked them they would shrink into little rubber balls.

- When I cook lobster and serve it with pasta, I want you to taste the lobster. Otherwise, why bother to use such an expensive ingredient? Lobster has a subtle, delicate taste that needs to be drawn out so it isn't overwhelmed by the pasta or the sauce. Again, I always keep the lobster in the shell.

- Rock shrimp is made to order to be cooked with pasta. It's a very forgiving protein—it's almost impossible to overcook and rubberize. When you cook them, you always end up with meaty shrimp and tons of shrimp flavor.

- Although it's not very popular to serve pasta with pieces of fish, I love it. When I was out on a boat in the Adriatic, that's what I would cook up every night. In some ways it's the most flavorful way to cook fish, plus it's really easy to eat. If you decide to go for it and cook pasta and seafood this way, be forewarned that it may be a tough sell for your guests. It usually works best with stewlike preparations, so the fish breaks down and gets incredibly tender.

- There are two dishes in this chapter that I created thinking about how you could substitute fish in a classic meat preparation. Everyone loves the Spaghetti with Tuna Meatballs on page 80, and I dare even the most devoted carnivore to resist the charms of that dish. And the Rigatoni with Tuna Bolognese (page 79) is just something I came up with when I had some extra tuna scraps that I wanted to use. I don't know that it's better than the classic Bolognese made with veal and pork, but it's certainly damn good in its own right.

Tagliatelle with Nantucket Bay Scallops

Simple pasta preparations like this are a nifty way to use delicious but expensive varieties of seafood cost-effectively. For one thing, you ensure that the seafood is the unquestioned star of the dish. Make sure you don't move the scallops at all after you put them in the sauté pan; if you do, you won't get that gorgeous, burnished brown crust we all love in sautéed scallops. Even more important, keep the scallops in the pan for no more than 30 seconds to prevent them from going Goodyear. You can also make this dish with Alaskan king or lump crabmeat, or with caviar (use the less expensive Mississippi paddlefish eggs), cooking the roe with a little pasta water or crème fraîche. Regardless of the seafood type, this is a fast-moving recipe, so have all your ingredients and equipment (colander and measuring cup) ready to go. **Serves 4**

$3/4$ **pound fresh tagliatelle**

$3/4$ **pound Nantucket Bay scallops**

Sea salt

Freshly ground black pepper

2 tablespoons plus $1/2$ cup extra-virgin olive oil

6 tablespoons unsalted butter, 2 tablespoons broken up into bits

Leaves from 12 sprigs chervil

Bring a large pot of salted water to a boil. Add the fresh pasta and cook for 3 minutes. Drain in a colander and reserve $1/2$ cup cooking liquid.

While the pasta is cooking, season the scallops on both sides with salt and pepper. Coat a large, preferably nonstick, sauté pan with 2 tablespoons olive oil. Heat the oil over a medium flame until it smokes. Add the scallops and distribute the 2 tablespoons broken-up butter around the pan. Count to 30 seconds, then shake the pan. Remove immediately and pour the contents of the pan onto a large platter. Set aside.

Return the pan to a medium-high flame. Add the pasta water, the drained pasta, and the remaining butter. Simmer until the liquid has almost disappeared. Turn off the flame and add the scallops (plus any liquid they may have given off) back to the sauté pan, along with the chervil. Add the remaining $1/2$ cup olive oil and toss to combine. Divide among four serving bowls and sprinkle each with some fine sea salt and freshly ground black pepper. Serve immediately.

Linguine with Clams, Pancetta, and Red Pepper Flakes

Depending on whom you talk to, linguine with clams is either an Italian restaurant classic or an Italian restaurant cliché. I avoid the cliché by improving on the classic: a little pancetta adds a deep layer of flavor, and the briny taste of mahogany clams brings a true taste of the ocean to the dish. For me, this is the epitome of simple coastal cooking. **Serves 4**

1 pound dried linguine

¼ cup plus 3 tablespoons extra-virgin olive oil, plus high-quality extra-virgin olive oil, for drizzling

1 clove garlic, thinly sliced

6 ounces pancetta, cut into thin strips

8 mild dried red chiles (such as Italian finger hots), whole

2¾ pounds clams (mahogany or littlenecks, about 48 total), scrubbed clean

⅓ cup dry white wine

1 cup Clam Stock or Lobster Stock (recipe follows) or pasta cooking water

½ teaspoon sea salt, plus more to finish

¼ teaspoon freshly ground black pepper, plus more to finish

1 teaspoon red pepper flakes

2 tablespoons chopped flat-leaf parsley

Bring a large pot of salted water to a boil. Add the linguine and cook for 1 minute less than the box directions (al dente—the pasta should still have bite to it). Drain in a colander, reserving 1 cup of the cooking liquid if not using the Clam Stock. Toss the pasta in the colander with ¼ cup of the olive oil, and set aside.

Heat 3 tablespoons of the olive oil in a 6-quart pot or Dutch oven with a lid over a medium-high flame. Add the garlic and pancetta and cook, stirring occasionally, until the garlic begins to take on color, about 4 minutes. Add the chiles and the clams, cover the pot, and cook until the clams begin to open, about 2½ minutes. Then add the wine and the Clam or Lobster Stock, or reserved pasta water (it should bubble when it hits the pan), and replace the lid. Cook for 2 to 3 minutes more, checking to see when all of the clams have opened (discard any that don't). Add the pasta and season with the ½ teaspoon salt and ¼ teaspoon freshly ground pepper. Add the red pepper flakes. Add the parsley, toss gently to combine, and cook for an additional minute or so to thoroughly reheat the linguine. Divide among four bowls, being sure to distribute the clams equally. Drizzle each bowl with a high-quality extra-virgin olive oil, a sprinkling of crunchy sea salt, and some freshly ground black pepper.

Clam Stock or Lobster Stock

Clam or Lobster Stock is a great ingredient to have on hand. It adds depth of flavor to just about any seafood dish, even one not made with clams. Clam or Lobster Stock also freezes well, so you can break it out when you need it. **Makes 1 quart**

1 tablespoon extra-virgin olive oil

2 shallots, chopped (about $^1/_2$ cup)

1 sprig thyme

4 black peppercorns

1 bay leaf

3 parsley stems

$1^2/_3$ cups dry white wine

4 pounds of chowder clams or 4 lobster bodies

Over a medium-low flame, heat the olive oil in a 4-quart pot. Add the shallots and cook slowly until translucent, about 5 minutes. Add the thyme, peppercorns, bay leaf, parsley stems, and white wine. Raise the flame to high, bring to a boil, and cook until the liquid reduces by half, about 7 minutes. Add the clams and enough water to completely cover them, about 1 quart. Bring to a boil, reduce the flame to medium, and cover. Simmer until all the clams have opened, about 6 minutes. (Discard any clams that don't open.) Strain the liquid through a fine-mesh sieve and discard the solids. Let the stock cool to room temperature before refrigerating. Clam or Lobster Stock can be refrigerated for up to 3 days, or frozen.

Shells

While a lot of people aren't used to a clam sauce arriving with the clams still in their shells, I wouldn't serve it any other way. Besides being more authentically Italian, and giving the finished dish more texture, an empty shell makes it easy to finish off whatever sauce remains in the bottom of the bowl—it works just like a spoon.

Spaghetti alla Chitarra with Sea Urchins & Crabmeat

Sea urchins, with their prehistoric-looking spiny shells, can be scary to the uninitiated. They have a lovely creamy flavor, but it's their orange color and custardy texture that seem to be the sticking points for a lot of people. I knew there might be some resistance to this dish when I put it on the menu at Esca, but it's turned into one of our signature dishes. The Sicilians love to use sea urchins in pasta preparations—the sea urchin's intensely flavorful, salty creaminess make it a perfect foil for pasta. In this recipe, the sweetness of the crab tempers the sea urchin's brininess, and makes the dish as much New York as Palermo. Here I use homemade pasta cut on taut strings (hence the name *chitarra*, Italian for guitar), because I like the slightly rough texture the strings create. But this dish will be just as delicious with a good dried spaghetti or linguine like Latini and DeCecco brand. **Serves 4**

1 pound dried spaghetti or chitarra

¼ cup plus 1 tablespoon extra-virgin olive oil

8 tablespoons (1 stick) unsalted butter

**8 ounces sea urchins
(2 trays of cleaned sea urchins)**

8 ounces jumbo lump crabmeat

½ teaspoon sea salt, plus more to finish

Freshly ground black pepper

Bring a large pot of salted water to a boil. Cook the pasta for 2 minutes less than the package instructs. Reserve 2 cups cooking water, and drain the pasta in a colander. Toss the cooked pasta with 3 tablespoons of the olive oil. Set aside.

Transfer the pasta water to a large, straight-sided sauté pan. Add the butter and bring to a boil over a high flame. Reduce the liquid by one quarter, about 3 minutes.

Add the pasta and toss to coat. Use a wooden spoon to push the pasta to one side of the pan, and add the sea urchins to the other side. Use the spoon to break up the flesh. Add the crabmeat, the remaining tablespoon olive oil, the ½ teaspoon sea salt, and several grindings of fresh pepper. Gently toss to combine.

Divide the pasta among four bowls, and season each serving with the sea salt and freshly ground pepper. Serve immediately.

"Catching a tuna is like trying to stop a VW bug going 60 miles an hour with a piece of string. I've fought tunas at 40 pounds and almost broke my back. I fought a **250-POUND TUNA** that really almost broke my back. Tuna sees light, he freaks— just when you think you got him, he can zing out a thousand yards of line."

Rigatoni with
Tuna Bolognese

I love a classic Bolognese sauce. But in a creative moment, I figured since
Esca is an Italian seafood restaurant, I might as well see what a Bolognese
sauce would taste like made with tuna instead of meat. I succeeded so well
that a lot of people can't tell the difference. That's because tuna is just as
meaty as beef, pork, or veal. Ask your fishmonger for tuna scraps when
you're making this dish. It will save you some money and you won't be
sacrificing anything in terms of flavor or texture. If you happen to own a
meat grinder, grind the tuna twice using a 1/4-inch die. **Serves 4**

**2 pounds fresh tuna scraps or steaks,
   cut into large chunks**

10 ounces pancetta, cut into medium dice

6 ounces mackerel, cut into large chunks

3 tablespoons olive oil

1 onion, diced

4 cloves garlic, crushed

One bottle (750-milliliter) red wine

1 bay leaf

1/2 cinnamon stick (about 2 inches)

1 teaspoon red pepper flakes

**One 28-ounce can whole peeled tomatoes
   (and their juice)**

Sea salt

Freshly ground black pepper

1 pound dried rigatoni (preferably DeCecco)

1/2 pound mascarpone cheese

In a food processor, pulse the tuna, pancetta, and mackerel until coarsely ground. Set
aside.

In a Dutch oven, heat the olive oil over a medium flame. Add the onion and
garlic and cook, stirring occasionally, until translucent, 3 to 4 minutes. Add the ground
tuna mixture, and increase the flame to medium high. Cook, stirring with a fork, until
all the juices are dry and the bottom of the pan begins to brown, 7 to 10 minutes. Add
the red wine, bay leaf, red pepper, and cinnamon stick, and cook until dry, about 15
minutes. Add the tomatoes, crushing them by hand, and their juice, and 1/2 cup water.
Season with 1 teaspoon salt and 1/2 teaspoon black pepper. Let simmer, uncovered, for
1 1/2 hours. The sauce should be moist, not wet. Taste and reseason with salt and
pepper. Discard the bay leaf and cinnamon stick.

Prepare the rigatoni according to package directions, cooking 1 minute less than
the package instructs for al dente. Drain in a colander and combine with the
Bolognese sauce. Divide among four serving bowls. Top each bowl with 1/4 cup of
mascarpone, a sprinkling of salt, and a grinding of pepper.

Spaghetti with Tuna Meatballs

I first had tuna meatballs at Bastanelli al Molo, a restaurant in a small town outside of Rome called Fiumicino. They were deliciously meaty (the pun—I know, I know), and I knew that when I got back to the States I was going to figure out how to make them at Esca. I'd love to make these at home with spaghetti all the time, but my wife Donna's family is Sicilian, so she doesn't believe in eating meatballs that she didn't make herself. There's one meatball maker in my house, and it isn't me. **Serves 4**

¾ cup bread cubes from a stale baguette	1 tablespoon chopped flat-leaf parsley
½ cup whole milk	¼ teaspoon red pepper flakes
5 tablespoons extra-virgin olive oil	Sea salt
2 cloves garlic, thinly sliced	Freshly ground black pepper
1½ pounds tuna, cut into 1-inch chunks	4 cups Basic Tomato Sauce (recipe follows)
2 ounces pancetta, finely diced (¼ cup)	1 pound dried spaghetti
1 large egg, lightly beaten	

Place the workbowl and blade of a food processor in the freezer. Soak the cubed bread in the milk for 30 minutes.

In a 9-inch sauté pan, heat 2 tablespoons of the olive oil over a medium flame. Add the garlic and cook until translucent, about 3 minutes. Set the pan aside to cool.

Squeeze the bread in your clean hands to remove excess milk, then transfer to the chilled workbowl. Add the tuna and pancetta. Pulse until just coarsely ground and combined. Place the workbowl in the refrigerator briefly to cool the tuna mixture.

Add the sautéed garlic and its oil to the chilled tuna-bread mixture. Add 2 tablespoons water, the egg, parsley, and red pepper flakes. Season with ½ teaspoon salt and a few turns of a pepper mill. Use your hands to lightly but thoroughly mix the ingredients until combined.

Over a low flame, heat the tomato sauce in a 6-quart pot.

Form the tuna mixture into twenty meatballs, each about 1¾ inches in diameter, or weighing about 1¼ ounces (see Preparation Note). Over a medium-high flame, heat the remaining 3 tablespoons olive oil (in the same pan that was used to sauté the garlic) until hot but not smoking. Cook the meatballs in three batches until well browned all around, 6 to 8 minutes. As they finish cooking, use a slotted spoon to transfer them to the simmering tomato sauce. When all of the meatballs have been transferred to the tomato sauce, partially cover the pot and gently simmer for 1 hour, carefully stirring occasionally.

Bring a large pot of salted water to a boil. Cook the spaghetti according to the instructions on the box, but 1 minute less than instructed for al dente. Drain the spaghetti and serve in a bowl with the sauce and meatballs spooned over, family-style.

PREPARATION NOTE

Before forming the entire batch into meatballs, I'll make one, sauté it, and then taste to correct the seasonings for the rest of the batch. This saves me from cooking all of the tuna and wishing it had more salt or more red pepper flakes. As always when making meatballs, the key is damp hands to keep the meatballs light and fluffy.

Basic Tomato Sauce

I learned this Basic Tomato Sauce from my mother-in-law, a serious Italian-American cook in her own right. Using extra-virgin olive oil in this recipe lends real character and depth of flavor. And don't skip the carrot—it gives sweetness without adding sugar. **Makes 5¾ cups**

¼ cup extra-virgin olive oil

2 cloves garlic, thinly sliced

½ onion, finely diced (about ½ cup)

1 carrot, finely diced (about ½ cup)

1 stalk celery, finely diced (about ½ cup)

One 28-ounce can San Marzano whole peeled tomatoes and their juices

1 tablespoon chopped basil leaves, with stems reserved

Sea salt

Freshly ground black pepper

Heat the olive oil in a 4- to 6-quart pot over a medium-low flame until hot but not smoking. Add the garlic and cook until soft and translucent, about 2 minutes. Add the onion, carrot, and celery and cook until soft, about 12 minutes, stirring occasionally.

Add the tomatoes and their juice. Use a fork or a whisk to break them up into chunks. Add the basil stems and simmer, stirring occasionally, until the tomatoes are soft and the sauce has thickened, about 45 minutes.

Stir in the chopped basil, and add a little salt and pepper. Remove from the flame and either use immediately or let cool and store covered in the refrigerator for up to 3 days; after that the sauce starts to taste like the fridge.

Above and right: Spaghetti with Lobster and Chiles (page 84)

Spaghetti with
Lobster & Chiles

This is a remarkably simple main-course pasta dish that I can't remove from the menu at Esca. The hot chiles play off the cool mint beautifully, and they complement the sweetness of the lobster meat. Don't be afraid to cook lobster at home. If you're squeamish about killing a live lobster, have your fishmonger kill and cut up the lobster for you. Just make sure you cook the lobster the day it's brought home from the fish market. **Serves 4 to 6**

Four 1-pound live lobsters

1 pound dried spaghetti

3 tablespoons extra-virgin olive oil, plus high-quality extra-virgin olive oil, for drizzling

2 cloves garlic, thinly sliced

1 to 3 diced serrano chiles, to taste (or poblano or jalapeño, depending on the amount of heat you prefer)

2 cups Basic Tomato Sauce (page 81)

10 mint leaves, rolled and finely sliced

Sea salt

Freshly ground black pepper

Bring a large pot of heavily salted water to a boil (the water should taste like the ocean) for the lobsters, and another pot of salted water to a boil for the pasta.

On a cutting board, hold the lobster facing your knife hand. Place the point of a very sharp chef's knife on the lobster's head just behind the eyes. Swiftly press the point in and bring the blade down to the cutting board, severing the head. The lobster will move and twitch, but it is no longer alive. Pull the claws from the body, using a slight twisting motion. Remove the tail: twist the tail in one direction and the body in the other. It should come apart cleanly. Set the tails aside.

Add the claws to the lobster pot and cook for 5 minutes (they will turn red). Use a slotted spoon to remove and let cool slightly. When cool enough to handle, cover with a kitchen towel and crack the claws by pressing down with a mallet or the handle of a chef's knife. Remove the meat from the claws and set aside in a bowl. Remove the meat from the knuckles (the segment between the claws and the body), and set aside in a separate bowl.

Cook the pasta for 1 minute less than the box directs for al dente. Reserve 1 cup of the cooking liquid and drain the spaghetti in a colander. Put the pasta in a bowl and toss with 1 tablespoon of the olive oil.

To cut the lobster tails in half lengthwise: place on a cutting board with the underside of the tail facing up. Use your body weight to press the blade into the tail, cutting through to the outer shell. Then cut across the tails so that each one is in four pieces.

In a large straight-sided sauté pan or in the pot used to cook the spaghetti, heat the remaining 2 tablespoons olive oil over a medium-high flame until smoking. Add the lobster tails and, stirring with a wooden spoon, cook until they start changing color, about 2 minutes. Add the garlic and chiles and cook until the garlic is translucent, about 1 minute. Add the cup of reserved pasta water, the tomato sauce, and the meat from the lobster claws. Simmer the sauce until it reduces slightly, about 4 minutes. Add the cooked pasta and the lobster knuckle meat, and toss with tongs to coat. Let the pasta reheat in the sauce for about a minute.

Serve the pasta in wide shallow bowls, being sure to evenly divide the lobster pieces. Drizzle with a high-quality extra-virgin olive oil and sprinkle with the fresh mint, sea salt, and pepper.

Photographs on pages 82–83

Tagliatelle with
Shrimp & Peas

There are few things better than fresh peas in spring, but frozen peas will work just fine in this dish. Sometimes, if they're really fresh and good, I don't even cook them when I make this dish—I just toss them in at the end. I like using fresh tagliatelle here, because of the way the sauce adheres to the fresh noodles. If you can't find fresh tagliatelle, fresh fettuccine will do. Shrimp and sweet peas are such a perfect combination, a culinary marriage made in heaven. And this dish is so easy to make, and so very tasty. **Serves 4 to 6**

1 pound fresh shelled peas (about 1¼ pounds before shelling), or frozen peas

4 ounces slab pancetta, cut into a small dice

1 pound medium shrimp (about 35 shrimp), peeled and deveined

Sea salt

Freshly ground black pepper

1 pound fresh tagliatelle or fettuccine

1 tablespoon roughly chopped tarragon leaves

½ cup extra-virgin olive oil, plus high-quality extra-virgin olive oil, for drizzling

Bring a large pot of salted water to a boil for the pasta, and a smaller saucepan of salted water to a boil for the peas.

Blanch the peas in the small saucepan until tender, approximately 5 minutes, depending on their size and starchiness—tasting them is the best gauge. Drain and set aside. (If using frozen peas, prepare them according to package instructions.)

In a large, straight-sided sauté pan, brown the pancetta over a medium flame, 5 to 7 minutes. Transfer the pancetta to a paper-towel-lined plate and set aside. Spoon some of the rendered fat out of the pan, leaving about 2 tablespoons.

Season the shrimp with salt and pepper. Add the shrimp to the pan and sauté for 5 to 6 minutes, turning them midway, until opaque. Turn off the flame, leaving the shrimp in the sauté pan.

Add the fresh pasta to the large pot of boiling water and cook for 1 minute less than the package instructs for al dente. Drain the pasta in a colander and add to the pan of shrimp. Return the pan to a medium flame, and add the blanched peas, pancetta, tarragon, and the ½ cup olive oil. Season with 1 teaspoon of sea salt and 1 teaspoon freshly ground black pepper; toss with tongs to fully combine. Divide the pasta in shallow bowls, and drizzle each bowl with high-quality olive oil, and finish with a sprinkling of coarse sea salt and freshly ground black pepper. Serve immediately.

Fettuccine with Shrimp and Radicchio

I like to serve this dish with head-on shrimp because they have a lot more flavor. But I realize that a lot of people don't want to wrestle with the shells, so you can shell them. Once again, I like the age-old combination of the bitter (radicchio) and the sweet (shrimp). Use either U12 (12 or fewer to the pound) or U10 shrimp here—big ones. When you buy the shrimp, make sure there is no discoloring of the shell; if the shell is black, the shrimp is too old to eat. **Serves 4 to 6**

1 pound fettuccine

¼ cup plus 3 tablespoons extra-virgin olive oil, plus high-quality extra-virgin olive oil, for drizzling

2 cloves garlic, minced

1 teaspoon red pepper flakes

1¼ pounds medium shrimp, peeled and deveined

1 medium head radicchio, core removed, leaves roughly chopped

Sea salt

Freshly ground black pepper

4 to 6 teaspoons *aceto balsamico* (aged balsamic vinegar)

Bring a large pot of salted water to a boil. Add the fettuccine and cook for 2 minutes less than the package directs (about 7 minutes). Drain in a colander, retaining ¼ cup cooking liquid. Put the pasta in a bowl and toss with 3 tablespoons of the olive oil.

In a large, straight-sided sauté pan over a medium-high flame, heat the ¼ cup olive oil until hot but not smoking. Add the garlic and red pepper flakes and cook for 2 minutes, stirring frequently. Add the shrimp and cook for 5 minutes, until opaque. Add the radicchio and sauté until it begins to wilt. Add the reserved ¼ cup pasta water and the fettuccine. Season with ½ teaspoon salt and ½ teaspoon black pepper. Cook for about 2 minutes more, tossing to combine the ingredients while the pasta water reduces.

Divide among wide, shallow bowls. Drizzle each serving with a generous amount of high-quality extra-virgin olive oil, a sprinkling of sea salt and freshly ground black pepper, and 1 teaspoon *aceto balsamico*.

Fettuccine with
Rock Shrimp,
Corn, & Jalapeño

Rock shrimp are delicious, forgiving, and so easy to cook with. How did I come up with this dish? I had all these "Biker Billy" jalapeños (a variety of large jalapeño that turns red upon ripening) in my garden one summer, and I wanted to do something with them in the restaurant. Peppers and corn are the essence of summer to me, and the jalapeños add just enough heat to make the dish interesting. I let the jalapeños turn red before using them so they are not super-spicy. This dish moves quickly, so set out all the ingredients before you begin. **Serves 4**

1 pound dried fettuccine

3 tablespoons plus ¼ cup extra-virgin olive oil, plus high-quality extra-virgin olive oil, for drizzling

1 medium jalapeño, stemmed and seeded, sliced in rounds

1 pound rock shrimp, peeled and deveined

Sea salt

Freshly ground black pepper

6 ears corn, kernels removed from cob (about 3 cups; see page 33 for technique)

2 cups arugula, rinsed and spun-dry, chopped

Bring a large pot of salted water to a boil. Add the fettuccine and cook 1 minute less than the box instructs for al dente. Drain the pasta in a colander, reserving about ¼ cup of the cooking water.

While the pasta is cooking, heat the 3 tablespoons olive oil over a medium flame in a deep, straight-sided sauté pan. Add the jalapeño and cook until softened, about 2 minutes. Season the rock shrimp with salt and pepper, then add to the pan. Sear the shrimp on all sides for 6 to 8 minutes total. Add the corn, stir well to combine, and cook for about 1 minute more. Season with ½ teaspoon sea salt.

Reduce the flame to medium and add the arugula. Stir to combine. Add the pasta and the reserved pasta water. Use tongs to combine the ingredients, and continue cooking for about 1 minute more. Season with additional salt and pepper. Use the tongs to transfer the pasta to four serving bowls, and drizzle some high-quality extra-virgin olive oil over each bowl before serving.

Fettuccine with
Rock Shrimp,
Cherry Tomatoes,
and Feta

I think this dish represents the essence of modern Italian cuisine. Traditionally, Italians didn't pair fish or shellfish with cheese, but these days you see it all over menus, both here and in Italy. For this dish, use the harder to find French feta (see Sources, page 237); it's less salty and creamier than its Bulgarian and Greek counterparts.

I also like making this dish with cherry tomato instead of plum tomato puree because even in New York you can get pretty good, sweet ones year-round. The number of jalapeños added depends on how much heat you and your dining companions like. **Serves 4**

1 pound rock shrimp, peeled and deveined

Sea salt

Freshly ground black pepper

3 tablespoons extra-virgin olive oil, plus high-quality extra-virgin olive oil, for drizzling

1 to 2 jalapeños, stemmed and seeded, cut into thin matchsticks

2 cloves garlic, thinly sliced

2 cups cherry tomato puree (see Sources, page 237)

1 pound fresh fettuccine

6 ounces mild feta (either French or Greek; see Sources, page 237)

Bring a large pot of salted water to a boil for the pasta.

Season the rock shrimp with salt and pepper. In a large, straight-sided sauté pan, heat the 3 tablespoons olive oil over a medium flame until hot but not smoking. Add the shrimp and sear on all sides, 6 to 8 minutes per side. Use a slotted spoon to transfer them to a plate. Add the jalapeño(s) and garlic to the pan and sauté for about 3 minutes, until they soften. Add the cherry tomato puree and season with $\frac{1}{2}$ teaspoon salt and 1 teaspoon pepper. Simmer over a low flame, until the tomato puree has thickened slightly, about 5 minutes.

Add the fettuccine to the boiling water. Cook for 1 minute less than the package directions instruct, then drain in a colander, reserving about ¼ cup cooking liquid. Add the fettuccine and the cooking liquid to the pan of simmering tomato puree and increase the flame to medium. Return the shrimp to the pan and toss to combine. Crumble the feta into the pan and continue gently to stir the pasta and sauce for about 1 more minute. Taste to see if the mixture needs more salt (the saltiness of the feta can vary).

Serve the pasta in four wide, shallow bowls with a drizzle of high-quality extra-virgin olive oil over the top of each serving along with some freshly ground black pepper.

Risotto with Lobster and Black Trumpet Mushrooms

I like my risotto wet for one simple reason: so that it stays moist until the last bite hits my tongue. Although other cooks may differ, I believe that Vilano nano rice from the Veneto region of Italy is the ideal rice to use in a risotto: it's hard to overcook, the grains don't clump together, and it has lots of flavor on its own. This particular risotto is a pretty dish, ideal for company—company you know well, however, because this is a rustic preparation that requires picking up the lobster pieces in the shell with your hands (don't forget to put bowls on the table for the empty shells). The sweet lobster meat adds a layer of rich, luxuriant flavor to the risotto, and the mushrooms lend a bit of earthy intensity. If you can't find black trumpet mushrooms, cultivated button mushrooms will work just fine. **Serves 4**

Two 1- to 1½ -pound lobsters

1 cup Lobster Stock or Clam Stock (page 75)

5 tablespoons extra-virgin olive oil

4 tablespoons unsalted butter

½ medium yellow onion, minced (about ¼ cup)

2 cloves garlic, minced

1½ cups Vilano nano or Arborio rice

½ cup dry white wine

1 pound black trumpet Braised Mushrooms, (recipe follows)

3 ounces Parmigiano-Reggiano, finely grated

Sea salt

Freshly ground black pepper

If you have live lobsters, follow the instructions on page 84 to kill them and take off the claws and tail. Cut the lobster tails into 4 pieces according to the instructions on page 85. Split each claw into 2 pieces.

Combine the Lobster Stock and 3/4 cup water in a saucepan. Bring to a low simmer.

In a Dutch oven, heat 2 tablespoons of the olive oil over a medium flame. Add 2 tablespoons of the butter. When the foam subsides, add the onion and garlic. Use a wooden spoon to thoroughly coat the garlic and onion with the olive oil and butter. Cook for 3 to 4 minutes, until the onion is translucent. Add the rice and stir constantly for about 2 minutes to lightly toast the rice (it should take on a little color).

Raise the flame to medium high and add the wine. Cook until the pan is nearly dry. Add a third of the simmering Lobster Stock to the rice and stir constantly until the liquid is almost completely absorbed. Add another third of the stock and continue stirring until the pan is nearly dry. Turn off the flame and place the lobster pieces, flesh down, in the rice. Cover the pot and let the lobster steam for 5 minutes.

Transfer the cooked lobster pieces to a bowl and return the flame to medium high. Add the remaining Lobster Stock and the Braised Mushrooms, and stir for 4 to 5 more minutes.

Add the remaining 3 tablespoons olive oil and butter, as well as the cheese, and stir until creamy. Season the risotto with salt and freshly ground black pepper. Serve in a wide shallow bowl, with the pieces of lobster on top. Self-service, family-style.

PREPARATION TIP

Make the Lobster or Clam Stock ahead of time. Use the bodies of the lobsters, reserving the claws and tails in the fridge. Let your fishmonger tear the lobsters apart for you.

Braised Mushrooms Serves 4

3 tablespoons extra-virgin olive oil

2 shallots, minced

2 tablespoons unsalted butter

1 cup dry white wine

1 sprig thyme

Salt

Freshly ground black pepper

1 pound mushrooms (black trumpets, chanterelles, morels, or cultivated button mushrooms)

Trace the diameter of a large straight-sided sauté pan on parchment paper and cut out the circle. This will serve as the pan's lid.

Heat the olive oil in the sauté pan over a medium flame until hot but not smoking. Add the shallots and cook, stirring occasionally, until soft and translucent, 4 to 5 minutes. Add the butter, wine, and thyme, and season with salt and pepper. Lower the heat to a gentle simmer, then add the mushrooms. Toss, then cover with the circle of parchment paper.

Cook the mushrooms at a low simmer for 30 minutes, stirring occasionally. They should be very tender. Season with more salt and pepper and serve immediately.

Whole-Wheat Spaghetti with
Fresh Sardines
and Walnuts

This is my version of a dish you find in every restaurant from Naples to Sicily. The pasta shape is Venetian, and the sauce is Sicilian. I have to thank cookbook writer and great Italian cook Arthur Schwartz for the addition of walnuts to this recipe, which add some crunchy earthiness to the dish. My Neapolitan-American neighbor Rosa also played a part: she showed me how to cook the tops and stems of the fennel. Use a good canned sardine packed in olive oil; I like the Agostino Recca brand. **Serves 4**

½ cup roughly chopped walnuts

1 head fennel, with fronds

¼ cup extra-virgin olive oil, plus high-quality extra-virgin olive oil, for drizzling

3 dried mild red chiles (such as Italian finger hot or red Thai chile)

4 cloves garlic, thinly sliced (2 tablespoons)

4 fresh sardine fillets with skin

1 cup Basic Tomato Sauce (page 81)

Sea salt

Freshly ground black pepper

8 ounces dried *bigoli* (whole-wheat spaghetti; see Sources, page 237)

Preheat the oven to 250°F.

Bring a large pot of salted water to a boil for the pasta. Spread the walnuts on a baking sheet, and toast for 3 to 5 minutes, until they give off an aroma. Set aside.

Remove the fennel fronds (the feathery green tops), roughly chop them, and set aside. Slice the bulb in half and remove the tough outer layer and core. Slice the rest of the bulb into thin matchsticks. Set aside.

Over a medium flame, heat the ¼ cup olive oil in a large sauté pan until hot but not smoking. Add the chiles and sliced garlic, and cook until the garlic is soft and translucent. Add the fennel and sauté until tender, 4 to 5 minutes. Add the sardine fillets and sauté for about 2 minutes, using a spoon to roughly chop the fillets in the pan. Add the walnuts and tomato sauce, and season with salt and pepper. Cook until the sauce has thickened, about 3 minutes. Turn off the flame.

While the sauce is thickening, add the pasta to the boiling water and cook for 1 minute less than the box directs. Strain in a colander. Add the pasta to the sauce and cook over a medium flame for 2 minutes, tossing the pasta to coat with the sauce.

Divide the pasta among four serving plates, drizzle with the high-quality extra-virgin olive oil, and garnish with the reserved fennel fronds.

Bucatini with Rita's Spicy Baby Octopus Sauce

I had the pleasure of cooking with Rita de Rosa while I was in Naples doing some research and development for Esca. Rita is a tiny, soulful woman with a big heart, and is a truly inspired Neapolitan cook. Like all great cooks, she is a very particular shopper. When she first showed me how to make this dish, we must have gone to ten markets before she found the octopus she liked. She always looked first at the number of suction cups on each tentacle, with three being the optimum number in her mind. She used bucatini, a fat, slightly rounded, long pasta, whose slight chewiness is an effective foil for the octopus. For those with an aversion to octopus, substitute medium shrimp (16 to 20 to a pound) or lump crabmeat. **Serves 4**

3 tablespoons extra-virgin olive oil, plus high-quality extra-virgin olive oil, for drizzling

2 cloves garlic, thinly sliced

4 whole dried arbol chiles

One 16½-ounce can whole peeled San Marzano tomatoes

1 pint cherry tomatoes

1½ pounds baby octopus, cleaned and cut into 2-inch pieces

Sea salt

½ teaspoon freshly ground black pepper

1 pound dried bucatini

¼ cup flat-leaf parsley, roughly chopped

Bring a large pot of salted water to a boil for the pasta.

Heat the 3 tablespoons olive oil in a large saucepan over a medium flame until hot but not smoking. Add the garlic and the chiles and sauté until the garlic begins to show color, about 4 minutes. Add the canned and fresh tomatoes and the octopus, and season with ½ teaspoon salt and the black pepper. Simmer, partially covered, using a fork occasionally to help break down the tomatoes, about 20 minutes. Remove the lid, raise the flame to medium high, and simmer briskly until the octopus is tender and the sauce has begun to thicken, about 7 minutes (but taste the octopus to be sure).

As soon as you remove the lid from the octopus, add the bucatini to the pot of boiling water and cook for 1 minute less than the box directs. Drain the pasta in a colander and add it to the saucepan. Toss the pasta and the sauce thoroughly to combine. Divide among four serving bowls, drizzle with high-quality extra-virgin olive oil, sprinkle with the parsley and additional sea salt, and serve immediately.

Chitarra with
Tuna Bottarga
and Bread Crumbs

My friend and business partner Molto (Mario Batali) taught me how to make this dish. *Bottarga* is the dried roe of either gray mullet or tuna. The eggs are removed immediately after the fish is caught, then they are pressed, sun-dried, and salted. The saline creaminess of the *bottarga* is a perfect foil for the crunch supplied by the bread crumbs. Mario grates the *bottarga*, while I like to shave it. Try it both ways and see which you prefer. **Serves 4**

1 pound chitarra or linguine

6 tablespoons extra-virgin olive oil, plus high-quality extra-virgin olive oil, for drizzling

2 cloves garlic, thinly sliced

4 tablespoons chopped flat-leaf parsley

1 teaspoon sea salt

1 teaspoon freshly ground black pepper

6 tablespoons Italian-Style Bread Crumbs (page 233)

6 ounces tuna *bottarga* (see Sources, page 237)

Bring a large pot of salted water to a boil. Add the pasta and cook for 1 minute less than the package instructions direct.

While the pasta is cooking, heat the 6 tablespoons olive oil in a large saucepan over a medium flame until hot but not smoking. Add the garlic and lightly brown, 4 to 5 minutes.

When the pasta is finished, drain and reserve 1 cup of the cooking liquid. Add the pasta and the cooking liquid to the sauté pan and raise the flame to medium high. Toss to combine the pasta with the olive oil and garlic while the liquid comes to a simmer. Cook for 45 seconds, then remove from the heat.

Add the parsley, salt, and pepper, and half the bread crumbs. Toss to combine. Divide the pasta into four serving bowls, drizzle with high-quality extra-virgin olive oil, and top with the remaining bread crumbs. Grate or shave the *bottarga* over each plate and serve.

Ricotta Gnocchi

There are just a few recipes in this book that don't include seafood. This is one of them. If I ever took these gnocchi off the menu at Esca, many of my regular customers would desert me; so in case I do, here's the recipe. The sheep's milk ricotta lends just the right amount of tang to these little dumplings. To get the feathery lightness everyone loves about these gnocchi, make sure you gently squeeze each of the mozzarella dough cubes to get as much of the water out of them as possible. And note that you should start the day before since the ricotta must be drained through cheesecloth. I always tell my cooks that well-made gnocchi should be light and fluffy, like a pillow, but they should never fall apart. **Serves 4**

1½ pounds sheep's milk ricotta

1 cup all-purpose flour

1 large egg, lightly beaten

3 tablespoons finely grated Parmigiano-Reggiano

Sea salt

Freshly ground black pepper

1¼ cups Basic Tomato Sauce (page 81)

1 tablespoon unsalted butter

4 ounces mozzarella di bufala, diced into ½-inch cubes

High-quality extra-virgin olive oil, for drizzling

Line a colander with a few layers of cheesecloth and place over a shallow bowl. Put the ricotta in the colander and then refrigerate overnight to drain the water from the cheese.

In the workbowl of a food processor, combine the ricotta, ½ cup of the flour, the egg, the Parmigiano-Reggiano, ½ teaspoon sea salt, and ½ teaspoon pepper. Pulse a few times to combine.

Transfer to a lightly floured board and knead in the remaining ½ cup flour. The dough will be sticky. Form into a ball, cover with plastic wrap, and refrigerate for at least 1 or up to 2 hours.

Line a baking tray with parchment.

Quarter the dough with a knife. With lightly floured hands and a well-floured board, roll one piece of dough into a 1-inch-thick rope. Cut the rope into 1-inch pieces. Use your thumb to gently press and roll the pieces into the back of a fork, lining and denting the gnocchi. Place on the prepared baking tray while the rest of the gnocchi are formed in the same way, using all of the dough.

Bring a large pot of salted water to a boil. Combine the tomato sauce and butter in a saucepan, and bring to a simmer.

Add the gnocchi to the boiling water. As they rise to the top of the pot, cook for an additional minute, then use a slotted spoon to transfer to the simmering sauce. Toss gently to coat the gnocchi with the sauce, and simmer for about 1 more minute. Remove the saucepan from the heat and season the sauce with additional salt and pepper. Gently squeeze the mozzarella cubes to remove any excess water before adding them to the sauce. Use two wooden spoons to gently toss and combine with the sauce. Divide among four plates and drizzle each with high-quality extra-virgin olive oil before serving immediately.

INGREDIENT NOTE

If sheep's milk ricotta isn't available, use ricotta *fresca*. Do not use the inferior-quality packaged variety.

Corkscrew Pasta with Scallops & Pesto

Coastal Liguria is the ancestral home of the classic pesto made with basil, pine nuts, garlic, and Pecorino Romano cheese. And although parts of Liguria are quite beautiful, its biggest city, Genoa, is industrial and not at all picturesque. Since much of Liguria hugs the coast, it only makes sense that Ligurians would marry pesto with scallops. It's worth it to use a good Pecorino Romano here (see Sources, page 237), and grate it yourself. Don't sear the pesto , or it will lose its aroma and color. I toss the boiled pasta and the finished pesto and then I throw in the just-sautéed scallops. **Serves 4 to 6**

1 pint cherry tomatoes, halved

½ cup Basil Pesto (recipe follows)

3 tablespoons plus ¼ cup extra-virgin olive oil

1 pound sea scallops

Sea salt

Freshly ground black pepper

1 pound corkscrew pasta

Bring a large pot of salted water to a boil for the pasta.

In a large mixing bowl, combine the halved cherry tomatoes with the pesto. Set aside.

Heat 3 tablespoons of the olive oil in a large sauté pan (preferably nonstick) over a medium-high flame until hot but not smoking. Dry the scallops with paper towels, then season both sides with salt and pepper. Add a scallop to the pan to test the heat (you should hear a sizzling sound); add the rest of the scallops to the pan and let them cook undisturbed before turning after 2 or 3 minutes. They should have a golden brown crust. Transfer the cooked scallops to a plate.

Add the pasta to the boiling water and cook for 1 minute less than the package directions direct.

Drain the pasta and add it to the pesto and tomatoes. Season with 1 teaspoon salt and ½ teaspoon pepper, and add the remaining ¼ cup olive oil. Toss to combine, add the scallops, and continue to mix. Spoon into serving bowls and enjoy.

Basil Pesto Makes 1 cup

I pair this classic Genovese pesto with scallops and corkscrew pasta, but it will also liven up tuna, swordfish, or any kind of meaty fish.

¼ **cup pine nuts**

2 **cloves garlic**

2 **teaspoons salt**

3 **cups basil leaves, well rinsed and spun-dry**

½ **cup extra-virgin olive oil**

¼ **cup finely grated Pecorino Romano or Parmigiano-Reggiano**

Preheat the oven to 300°F.

Spread the pine nuts on a baking sheet. Toast the nuts in the oven until aromatic and lightly colored, about 3 minutes.

Place the garlic cloves in a mortar (or blender or food processor) and add the salt and pine nuts. If using a mortar and pestle, pound after each addition; if using a blender or food processor, pulse to combine well.

Add the basil and continue to process to a vivid green paste. Add the olive oil gradually and then the grated cheese and process a final time to combine.

Use immediately or store in an airtight container in the refrigerator. If making ahead, drizzle some additional olive oil over the pesto to help it keep its color.

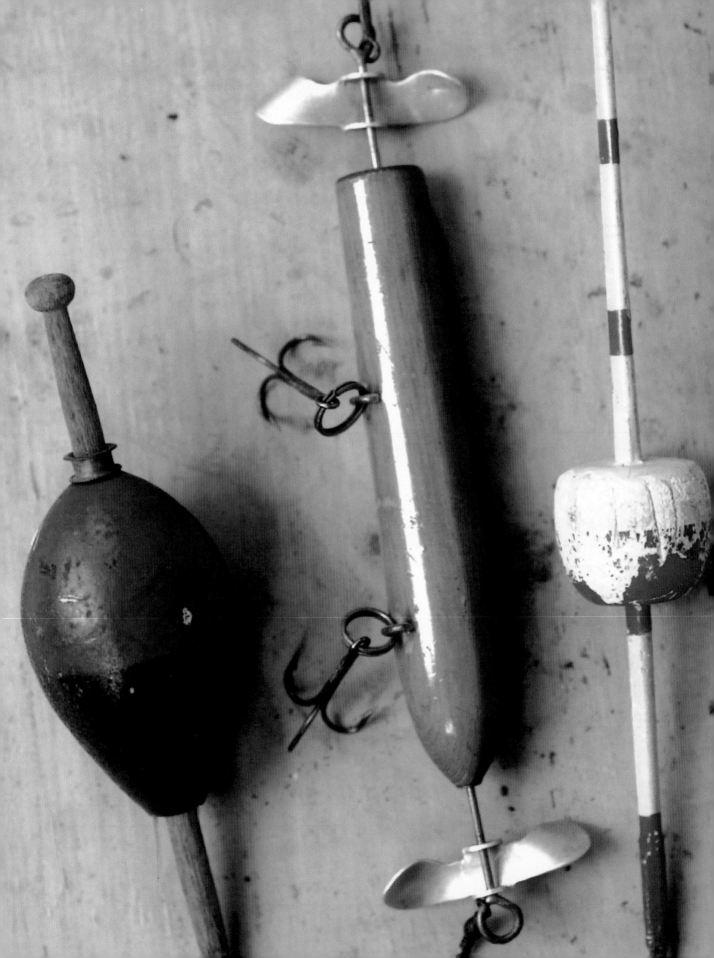

Grillin', Gillin', & Chillin'

My idea of a perfect summer Sunday: I'm in my little backyard grilling some fish I caught the day before, surrounded by family and friends, drinking a beer or a glass of wine, swapping fish tales. Here are my tips on how to make the best of that:

• I like the flavor that natural hardwood charcoal imparts to food (to fish and shellfish in particular). It burns faster and cleaner than charcoal briquettes. It's more expensive, but it's worth it. Even though gas grills work just fine with all these recipes—I have cooked on them many times, and I appreciate how easy they are to use—I just prefer hardwood charcoal.

• There is no better, simpler, cheaper method to start your fire than an old-fashioned metal chimney. Just ball up three or four sheets of newspaper, stuff them in the bottom cage of the chimney, pour your hardwood charcoal in, and light the newspaper in three places. Fifteen minutes later, you have a great fire to cook on.

• Be sure that when you pour the charcoal out of the chimney onto the grill that you are wearing oven mitts and shoes. I have given myself a hot foot more times than I can count.

• Spread the coals evenly across the diameter of the grill. There should be two sections of coals. When you dump the first group into the fire, the coals should be on their way to being white-hot, the point at which you get the least amount of flame flare-up. Light the second section five minutes after the first, to feed the main fire in case the heat begins to drop.

• Having two sections of coals of course means having two chimney starters—but at $15 or $20 a pop, that shouldn't break the bank.

• The fish should not go straight from the fridge onto the grill. Let the fish stand at room temperature for 30 to 60 minutes, depending on the size of the fish.

• The grill should be very hot before the fish goes on.

• This is very important: the fish should sit undisturbed for at least four minutes before turning, so that it doesn't stick and so that you get the nice caramelized, charred crust everyone loves to have on grilled fish.

Tuna on a Plank

Baking fish on a plank was a technique that Native Americans taught the early colonists. The plank, usually made of cedar, gives food a unique wood-smoky flavor that doesn't overpower it. Although you most commonly see salmon cooked by this method, I like to cook bluefin or big eye tuna this way. They're two of the richer, fattier tuna species, and they take to plank cooking in a big way. Soak your planks overnight to avoid any potential safety hazards. Serve this succulent tuna with Three-Bean Salad (page 129) or an heirloom tomato salad (page 18). **Serves 4**

4 tuna steaks (about 6 ounces each), 1¾ inches thick
Sea salt
Freshly ground black pepper

12 slices pancetta or double-thick bacon
2 lemons, cut into wedges
High-quality extra-virgin olive oil, for drizzling

Prepare 4 cedar planks according to the package instructions (which will probably mean: soak them overnight in water).

Prepare the charcoal fire. Preheat the grill over it as well as the cedar planks.

Season the fish with salt and pepper and drape three slices of pancetta over each tuna steak.

When the coals are red-hot, with some flame left to them, place the tuna on the planks on the grill. The boards will begin to smolder. Cook the steaks until they flake when you press your finger into them, 12 to 15 minutes.

Serve the tuna steaks hot off the grill or at room temperature, with plenty of lemon wedges and a drizzle of high-quality extra-virgin olive oil.

Grilled Porgy

with Salsa Verde and Braised Carrots

Salsa Verde (green sauce) is highly acidic, clean, and fresh-tasting. It tastes good on just about anything. It also happens to be the perfect complement to a rich fish like porgy, an inexpensive variety that I love, though in Italy a whole grilled fish is served plain. Any fish with a hearty skin will work here, like a Mediterranean snapper or arctic char, as it has to hold up to the grill's intense heat. *Note:* The recipe below, using one whole porgy, serves two people. **Serves 2**

FOR THE SALSA VERDE

2 tablespoons coarse sea salt

3 sprigs rosemary, needles picked off the stems

2 anchovy fillets

1 clove garlic

½ cup chives, cut into 1-inch pieces

1 cup fennel tops, fronds picked off the stems

6 sprigs tarragon, leaves picked off the stems

3 sprigs oregano, leaves picked off the stems

1 cup extra-virgin olive oil

Juice of ½ lemon (about 1½ tablespoons)

Sea salt

Freshly ground black pepper

FOR THE PORGY

One 2-pound porgy, scales and fins removed and gutted

4 parsley stems

2 medium lemon slices

1 clove garlic, crushed

Extra-virgin olive oil, to coat the fish

Sea salt

Freshly ground black pepper

Braised Carrots (recipe follows)

MAKE THE SALSA VERDE

Use a mortar and pestle, combine the sea salt and rosemary and crush to a fine dust.

Add the anchovies and garlic, and continue pounding until the mixture has the consistency of a paste. Follow with the chives, fennel tops, tarragon, and oregano, pounding after each addition. Transfer the paste to a small mixing bowl and add the olive oil and lemon juice. Taste and then adjust the seasoning by adding salt and pepper as needed. This should be made shortly before serving so the herbs are still fresh tasting. Leftovers can be refrigerated and brought to room temperature before serving as a condiment.

MAKE THE PORGY

Prepare a charcoal fire and let the grill get very hot.

continued

Dry the fish with paper towels. Stuff the cavity with the parsley stems, lemon slices, and garlic. Rub the fish on both sides with olive oil and season with salt and pepper.

When the coals are white-hot, place the fish over the medium-high part of the fire (where you can hold your hand above the coals for, say, 4 seconds). If the flames jump to touch the fish, move it to a cooler part of the grill. Grill the fish for 8 to 10 minutes per side. The skin should be charred but not blackened. The flesh of the fish, when touched, should gently break away under the skin.

Fillet the fish (see page 113) and transfer to two serving plates. Spoon a tablespoon of the *Salsa Verde* over each piece just before serving with the Braised Carrots.

Braised Carrots

Braising, which concentrates and intensifies the carrots' flavor, is my favorite way of cooking them. (You can also serve them with sautéed scallops, a poached halibut fillet, or even a pork roast.) **Serves 4**

3 tablespoons extra-virgin olive oil

2 shallots, thinly sliced

1½ cups moscato wine

2 cups orange juice

⅓ cup light brown sugar

3 cups baby carrots

3 sprigs thyme

Sea salt

Freshly ground black pepper

4 tablespoons unsalted butter

Heat the olive oil in a sauté pan over a medium flame until hot but not smoking. Add the shallots and cook until translucent, about 3 minutes. Add the moscato, orange juice, and brown sugar, raise the heat, and bring to a simmer.

Add the carrots and the thyme, stir thoroughly, and cover. Cook the carrots until they're almost tender, about 15 minutes. Remove the lid and let the liquid evaporate until the pan is moist but no longer wet. Remove the thyme sprigs. Season with salt and pepper, add the butter, stir until it melts, and transfer the carrots to a serving bowl.

Swordfish
with Almonds

In Sicily, there are almond trees everywhere, and tons of swordfish. I tend to serve swordfish only when it is being fished locally (for me, that is) in the North Atlantic. But good swordfish is available year-round from the Gulf of Mexico, Florida, and even South Africa. And although it was at one point an endangered species, there are now plenty of (sword) fish in the sea. When you buy swordfish, the flesh should be a rosy color, not white. Look for swordfish steaks that have little or no white cartilagenous fiber and no blemishes. To get the desired texture for the crust, crush the almonds by hand (in a mortar and pestle or on a cutting board), not in a food processor. Then toast them in a pan until they're brown while making sure they don't burn. **Serves 4**

1 cup blanched whole almonds

Four 6-ounce swordfish steaks, about 1¾ inches thick

Extra-virgin olive oil

Sea salt

Freshly ground black pepper

Sautéed Spinach (page 180)

Preheat the oven to 300°F.

Crush or roughly chop the blanched almonds. Spread the almonds on a baking sheet and toast for 3 to 4 minutes, until fragrant and lightly browned. The almonds should take on some color, but watch carefully so they don't burn.

Prepare a charcoal fire and heat the grill over it.

Brush both sides of the swordfish steaks with olive oil and season with salt and pepper. Grill the swordfish over a medium-high flame until the flesh starts to flake when you press it with your finger, about 6 minutes per side.

Serve the steaks with a heap of Sautéed Spinach alongside, and the crushed almonds sprinkled over the top.

Grilled Snapper

with Almond-Oregano Pesto

The Sicilians grow almonds and oregano, and they use them together in many dishes. So I started playing around with the two ingredients after a recent trip to Sicily, and this recipe is the result. Unlike Genovese pesto, this one contains no cheese. If you want to sweeten the dish just a tad, use orange juice instead of lemons. You can also substitute pine nuts or hazelnuts for the almonds, and the dish will turn out just as well. But walnuts might be a little too pungent and earthy. *Note:* The recipe serves two people. **Serves 2**

One 2-pound snapper, scales and fins removed, gutted
4 parsley stems
2 slices lemon
1 clove garlic, crushed

¼ cup extra-virgin olive oil
Sea salt
Freshly ground black pepper
Almond-Oregano Pesto (recipe follows)

Prepare a charcoal fire and heat the grill over it.

Dry the fish with paper towels. Stuff the cavity with the parsley stems, lemon slices, and garlic. Rub the fish on both sides with olive oil (use about 2 tablespoons per side) and season with salt and pepper.

When the coals are white-hot, place the fish over the medium-high part of the fire (where you can hold your hand above the coals for, say, 4 seconds). If the flames jump to touch the fish, move it to a cooler part of the grill. Grill the fish for 8 to 10 minutes per side. The skin should be charred but not blackened. The flesh of the fish, when touched, should gently break away under the skin.

Fillet the fish (see opposite) and transfer to two serving plates. Spoon a few tablespoons of the pesto over each piece just before serving.

Almond-Oregano Pesto Makes 1¼ cups

¾ cup blanched whole almonds

2 cloves garlic

1 fresh anchovy fillet

1 tablespoon coarse sea salt,
    plus additional for finishing

1 cup oregano leaves

¼ cup lemon juice

¼ cup freshly squeezed blood orange juice

¾ cup extra-virgin olive oil

Freshly ground black pepper

Toast the almonds according to the directions on page 111. Using a mortar and pestle or a small food processor, pound or process the nuts to small pieces (but not a powder). Transfer to a small mixing bowl and set aside.

Combine the garlic, anchovy fillet, and 1 teaspoon of the salt and pound into a paste. Add the oregano leaves ¼ cup at a time along with one quarter of the remaining salt each time. Continue to pound the ingredients to a fine paste. Add the paste to the almonds, stirring to combine. Add the lemon juice, blood orange juice, and olive oil, and combine well. Season with salt and freshly ground black pepper.

Use immediately or store in an airtight container in the refrigerator. If making ahead, drizzle some additional olive oil over the pesto to help it keep its color.

How to Fillet a Whole Fish

At Esca the waiters fillet a whole fish tableside. Here's the way to do it at home.

When the fish is done, the skin will usually have begun to split down the back. Insert a sauce spoon or a table knife into this split (or, if necessary, use the spoon or knife to split the skin) and slide the spoon or knife under the top fillet and over the bones all the way down to the belly. Use the side of the spoon or the knife blade to separate the top fillet from the head (just behind where the pectoral fin would be), then flip the top fillet onto the side of the plate or transfer it to a serving plate. Lift up and remove the spine from the bottom fillet. Then use the edge of the spoon or the knife blade to separate the bottom fillet from the head; leave it on the plate, or transfer it to the serving plate.

Sicilian-Style Swordfish

I got this idea watching a really good Sicilian home cook actually roll the swordfish in bread crumbs before she grilled it. I was in Taormina with one of Esca's winemakers, and his mom insisted on cooking for us. I had never seen that technique before, but you end up with a piece of fish with great crunchy texture and a lovely smoky flavor. The bread crumbs soak up all the juices, and the olive oil binds them to the fish. If you use a steel pan you are less likely to burn the bread crumbs. Serve with heirloom tomato salad (page 18). **Serves 4**

Four 6-ounce swordfish steaks, about 1¾ inches thick (see Ingredient Note)
Extra-virgin olive oil
Sea salt

Freshly ground black pepper
2 cups Italian-Style Bread Crumbs (page 233)
2 lemons, cut into wedges

Prepare a charcoal fire and heat the grill over it.

Dry the swordfish steaks with paper towels. Brush them on both sides with extra-virgin olive, season with salt and pepper, then dredge in the bread crumbs.

Place the fish over the medium-hot part of the fire and grill until the bread crumbs turn golden, no less than 5 minutes per side; if they begin to toast too quickly, move the fish to a cooler part of the grill. The cooked swordfish should be golden brown and the flesh should begin to flake when you press it with your finger.

Serve immediately with wedges of lemon.

INGREDIENT NOTE
Buy larger-sized swordfish steaks so they can be cut thicker—in other words, instead of asking for four 6-ouncers, ask for two 12-ouncers, and then have your fishmonger slice them into individual portions. The steaks should be about 1¾ to 2 inches thick.

Grilled Red Snapper
with Peperonata

This recipe is not for beginners. (If you ski, this is my double-black-diamond recipe.) Grilling delicate fillets is a practiced art, one that you can master only by trial and error. The fillets should come from a larger red snapper, so that they are about $1\frac{1}{4}$ inches thick at the thickest part. Prepare this unusual peperonata ahead of time. Serve it hot or at room temperature. **Serves 4**

FOR THE PEPERONATA

Extra-virgin olive oil

1 garlic clove, crushed

1 large yellow onion, cut into a medium dice

1 large fennel bulb, cut into a medium dice

2 red bell peppers, cut into 2-inch matchsticks

2 yellow bell peppers, cut into 2-inch matchsticks

2 orange bell peppers, cut into 2-inch matchsticks

1 hot pepper, seeded and cut into thin matchsticks

2 bay leaves

1 sprig fresh rosemary, needles roughly chopped

Sea salt

Freshly ground black pepper

FOR THE SNAPPER

Four 6-ounce red snapper fillets, skin on

Extra-virgin olive oil, to coat the fish, plus high-quality extra-virgin olive oil, for drizzling

Sea salt

Freshly ground black pepper

$\frac{1}{4}$ cup oil-cured olives, pitted and cut in half

MAKE THE PEPERONATA

Over a medium-high flame, heat the olive oil in a straight-sided skillet. Add the garlic and cook for about 2 minutes to soften. Add the onion and cook, stirring frequently, until translucent, about 7 minutes. Add the fennel, all the bell peppers, the hot pepper, bay leaves, and rosemary, and salt and pepper to taste. Cook until the vegetables are very soft and limp, with no crunch left in them, about 20 minutes. Store the peperonata at room temperature until ready to use, or refrigerate in a sealed container for up to 3 days.

Reheat in a saucepan, with a little olive oil, before using.

MAKE THE SNAPPER

Place the fillets, skin side down, on paper towels.

Prepare a charcoal fire and heat the grill over it.

Rub both sides of the fillets with olive oil and season the flesh side with salt and pepper. Place the fillets, skin side down, on the hot grill over medium-high heat. Grill them for 4 or 5 minutes, so that the skin side is well grilled and the flesh is beginning to cook but is still moist and not yet flaky. Carefully turn the fillets and grill the flesh side for just about 1 minute.

To serve the fillets, divide them among four plates. Place each fillet over a few spoonfuls of warm peperonata and a few olives. Top with a drizzle of top-quality extra-virgin olive oil, and season with salt and pepper.

"This morning I went out fishing with Artie for **MAKO SHARK.** I sat for an hour waiting for a bite. It was like oceanic meditation. Then I got one on the line, and I tell you, this shark was a **ROUGH HOMBRE.** He put up a wicked fight. Mako sharks are not exactly user-friendly. Have you ever seen an angry mako? **IT'S NOT PRETTY."**

Mako
with Jerusalem Artichoke Puree and Oven-Dried Tomatoes

Mako is an underrated fish. Sure, it's a shark, but it's not like eating Jaws. A piece of mako has a buttery, steaklike texture and a mild flavor. Ask for the belly cut, the thicker the better, so the steaks can get nice and caramelized on the grill. In fact, this is a good recipe to break out the grill pan if you don't want to fire up your outdoor grill. Jerusalem artichokes taste more like a nutty potato than an artichoke. A little vin cotto (cooked wine), or some reduced balsamic vinegar lends this dish sweetness.

Serves 4

Jerusalem Artichoke Puree (recipe follows)
Four 6-ounce mako steaks, about 2 inches thick
Extra-virgin olive oil
Sea salt

Freshly ground black pepper
8 Oven-Dried Tomatoes (page 205),
    warm or at room temperature, cut in half

Prepare a charcoal fire and heat the grill over it. Heat the Jerusalem Artichoke Puree over a very low flame.

Rub the mako on both sides with olive oil and season both sides with salt and pepper. Grill the fish for about 5 minutes per side, so the outside is well charred. The flesh of the fish should flake away when you press your finger into it.

To serve, spoon a few tablespoons of the Jerusalem Artichoke Puree into the center of four serving plates. Place the mako steaks on the puree and then surround each with four halves of Oven-Dried Tomatoes. Serve immediately.

Jerusalem Artichoke Puree

This preparation takes a fairly obscure root vegetable and makes it into a creamy alternative to mashed potatoes. **Makes 1½ cups**

Juice of 1 lemon

1 tablespoon salt, plus more to taste

3 pounds medium Jerusalem artichokes

2 tablespooons extra-virgin olive oil, plus more as necessary

Freshly ground black pepper to taste

Fill a stockpot or Dutch oven with water (about three-quarters full) and add the lemon juice and 1 tablespoon of salt. Scrub and peel the Jerusalem artichokes and place them in the water. Over a high flame, bring the pot to a boil and cook until the artichokes are tender, about 20 minutes. Strain in a colander. Transfer them to a food processor, add the olive oil, and pulse until smooth, adding more oil if necessary to achieve a smooth consistency. Season with salt and pepper and serve immediately.

Artie's
Seafood Market

Artie Hoenig is one of my best fishing buddies, and he also supplies me with a lot of great fish for the restaurant. Porgys, bluefish, tuna, striped bass, just about every local fish on the menu at Esca has at one time or another been caught and supplied by Artie. In my town Artie owns a seafood market and restaurant, Artie's Seafood Market. He opened in 1974 and often sells and serves fish that he has caught with me on his commercial boat. The market is a family affair. Artie's nephew shucks clams, his daughters wait on tables, and his wife manages the dining room. Artie's fried clams are good (he shucks the clams to order), but they're not like the clams I fry at Esca. He uses huge local clams that he leaves the neck on. It makes his clams a little chewy but really good.

Artie opened the market after a failed attempt at corporate life. His cousin offered him a job at his PR firm in Manhattan. Artie hated every minute of it. One early evening during Christmas week Artie was in Penn Station waiting for the train. They announced the train was being cancelled. The people on the platform were ten deep. He couldn't move. He told me he felt like he was in a cattle car. That was the last day for him working that job.

Now Artie's been stinking like a dead fish for twenty-nine years. The man doesn't cheat anybody. Between fishing and running the market and restaurant, he works eighteen hours a day. Artie makes an honest living selling honest food and fantastic fresh fish. Plus, the man's always up for fishing, any time of the day and any time of the year. Almost every day the phone rings at my home or at the restaurant and it's Artie asking me if I want to go fishing. He tells me and my wife the same thing every time: "I'll have you back by six."

Grilled Tuna
and Panzanella

Panzanella is the classic Tuscan salad of day-old bread and tomatoes that, when made properly, ends up wet and vinegary yet still crunchy. The best one I've ever had was in Porto Ercules, a cute little fishing village. For this dish I use local heirloom tomatoes that I either grow myself in my little garden or buy from my main tomato guy, Tim Starks. You don't have to use heirloom tomatoes, but for this dish I would definitely use vine-ripened tomatoes. Cardboardy, tasteless out-of-season tomatoes that have been picked green, gassed to turn red, and then trucked hundreds or thousands of miles will have a seriously deleterious effect on this dish. But feel free to substitute swordfish for the tuna. **Serves 4**

1 loaf rustic peasant bread, crusts removed

Extra-virgin olive oil

Sea salt

Freshly ground black pepper

$1/3$ cup Chianti vinegar

1 red bell pepper

1 yellow bell pepper

2 large heirloom or vine-ripened beefsteak tomatoes, cut into chunks

1 pint cherry tomatoes, halved

6 plum tomatoes, cut into spears

1 large or 2 medium cucumbers, peeled, seeded, and diced

1 small red onion, diced (about $1/4$ cup)

$1/4$ cup capers (preferably salt-packed)

$1/4$ cup pitted Gaeta olives

$1/4$ cup basil leaves (preferably opal basil)

$1/4$ cup flat-leaf parsley leaves

Four 6-ounce tuna steaks, about $1^3/4$ inches thick

Preheat the oven to 250°F.

Cut the bread into large ($1^1/2$ to 2 inch) cubes; you should have at least twenty-four croutons. Place the cubes on a baking sheet and drizzle with olive oil. Season with salt and pepper and place in the oven until the bread is dry and crunchy, about 30 minutes. (These can be made a day ahead and kept in a paper bag.)

Combine the Chianti vinegar with $2/3$ cup olive oil. Season with $1/2$ teaspoon salt and $1/2$ teaspoon black pepper. Set aside.

Roast the peppers over an open flame; this can be done directly on the stove top over a burner or over a charcoal fire. Turn the peppers so that the skin blackens and blisters all the way around. Put the roasted peppers in a bowl and cover with plastic wrap (the heat will help steam off the skin). When they are cool enough to handle, use your fingers to peel away the charred skin. Cut the peppers in half, remove the seeds, and then dice. Set aside.

Place all the cut-up tomatoes in a colander over a bowl for about an hour to drain off some of their liquid. Meanwhile, in a large mixing bowl, combine the diced peppers, cucumber, red onion, capers, olives, basil, and parsley.

Start a charcoal fire, heating the grill over it so that it's very hot.

Rub the tuna steaks on both sides with olive oil and season with salt and pepper. When the coals are white-hot, place the fish over the medium-high part of the fire (where you can hold your hand above the coals for, say, 4 seconds). If the flames jump to touch the fish, move them to a cooler part of the grill. Grill the fish for 5 to 6 minutes per side. When finished, the fish should feel like the fleshy part of your palm. Transfer the cooked fish to a serving platter.

Add the tomatoes and the croutons to the salad ingredients. Whisk the reserved oil and vinegar, and dress the salad, tossing gently but thoroughly. Serve the salad on a platter rather than in a bowl (the weight of the tomatoes can be crushing). Self-service, family-style.

Salmon with Figs, Saba, and Watercress

This dish is well served by using a grill pan, because the figs get caramelized from the saba. I serve it with wild watercress, which is spicy and very bitter, but cultivated watercress might work better for some people. Saba is grape must (cooked juice) made from the same Trebbiano grape used for balsamic vinegar; it tastes like Italian maple syrup. If you can't find saba in your gourmet grocery, use balsamic vinegar. This dish calls for fresh figs rather than dry, and if you'd rather sauté the salmon, you can throw the cut-up figs into the same pan. **Serves 4**

2 tablespoons saba or top-quality balsamic vinegar

½ cup extra-virgin olive oil, plus more for coating the salmon

Sea salt

Freshly ground black pepper

2 bunches watercress, rinsed and spun-dry

Four 6-ounce salmon fillets, skin on

8 ripe figs, halved

In a small bowl, whisk together the saba and the ½ cup olive oil and season with about ½ teaspoon salt and a pinch of black pepper. Put the watercress in a mixing bowl, add some dressing, and toss to coat. Divide the salad among four plates.

Preheat a grill pan over a medium-high flame.

Rub the salmon fillets on both sides with olive oil and season with salt and pepper. Place skin side down in the pan and cook until the edges of the fish begin to turn opaque, 4 to 5 minutes. Turn the fillets and cook 1 minute more. Transfer them to the serving plates, skin side down, over the watercress.

Place the figs in the grill pan, moving them around gently until they begin to wilt, about 2 minutes. Arrange the figs on each serving plate (four halves per plate) and drizzle them with whatever saba vinaigrette remains in the mixing bowl. Finish with a sprinkling of salt and black pepper. Serve immediately.

Grilled Mahimahi
with Panella and Chickpeas

Panella are amazingly delicious chickpea fritters that are found all over Sicily. I shallow-fry mine in olive oil until they're crispy on the outside and soft and gooey on the inside. In this dish I also use chickpeas (fresh or canned) in a salad with olives, oven-dried tomatoes, and arugula. Mahimahi is one of those great eating fish that even nonfish lovers swoon over. When fresh, it's a meaty, clean-tasting fish. I've caught a lot of mahimahi in my day in Florida. They don't play hard to get. In fact, I would have to say that mahimahi are pretty stupid. You catch one and you reel it halfway into the boat, and the others follow. **Serves 4**

FOR THE CHICKPEAS

1 cup dried chickpeas (see Preparation Note)

2 ounces pancetta, unsliced

1 small carrot, roughly chopped

1 small yellow onion, quartered

$\frac{1}{2}$ stalk celery

Extra-virgin olive oil

Salt

Freshly ground black pepper

1 cup roughly chopped arugula

FOR THE PANELLA

1 cup whole milk

$1\frac{1}{3}$ cups chickpea flour, plus more for dusting the work surface

Sea salt

Freshly ground black pepper

1 teaspoon garlic oil (see page 162) or olive oil

FOR THE MAHIMAHI

Extra-virgin olive oil, plus high-quality extra-virgin olive oil, for drizzling

Four 6-ounce mahimahi steaks, approximately $1\frac{3}{4}$ inches thick

Sea salt

Freshly ground black pepper

MAKE THE CHICKPEAS

Soak the chickpeas overnight (or up to 2 days) in water.

Preheat the oven to 350°F.

Drain the chickpeas and rinse in a colander. Transfer to a large ovenproof saucepan with a tight-fitting lid. Add the pancetta, carrot, onion, and celery. Add enough water to cover by 2 inches. Bring to a boil over a high flame, then cover the pot and transfer to the oven. Cook until the beans are tender, 2 to 3 hours (the cooking time varies depending on the beans). Check the beans periodically and add more water if neccessary, tasting them to gauge how tender they are. Remove from the heat and discard the vegetables. Drain. Dress the beans with olive oil, salt, and pepper.

The chickpeas can be made ahead, refrigerated, and then reheated (in a saucepan) just before you put the fish on the grill.

MAKE THE PANELLA

Combine the milk with 1 cup water in a medium saucepan. Bring to a simmer, then reduce the flame to low. Sift the chickpea flour into the simmering liquid and whisk immediately to combine, using a rubber spatula to scrape down the sides of the pot. Season with salt and pepper to taste and resume whisking. Remove the pan from the stove and continue to whisk. The batter should be thick—somewhere between pancake batter and brownie batter lies panella; add additional water if necessary. Add the garlic oil and 3 tablespoons water, and cook a few minutes more.

Pour the batter into a nonstick 9 x 13-inch cake pan and cover with a square of parchment paper. There should be enough batter to make at least 12 fritters. Refrigerate at least 2 hours or overnight.

PREPARE THE MEAL

Lightly dust a work surface with chickpea flour. Turn the cake pan onto the surface and either use a ring mold to cut out disks, or cut the chilled batter into squares.

Lightly coat a nonstick pan with olive oil, and heat until hot but not smoking. Pan-fry the chickpea pancakes until lightly golden, 3 to 4 minutes per side. Transfer to a plate lined with paper towels.

Prepare a charcoal fire and heat the grill over it.

If you refrigerated the chickpeas, begin reheating them over a low flame. Use a fork to mash a few of them and add enough olive oil to moisten them. Add the roughly chopped arugula leaves, stir to combine, and leave over a very low flame to keep warm.

Rub the mahimahi with olive oil and season on both sides with salt and pepper.

When the coals are white-hot, place the fish over the medium-high area (where you can hold your hand above the coals for 4 seconds). If the flames jump to touch the fish, move them to a cooler part of the grill. Grill for 4 to 5 minutes per side.

When finished, the fish should feel like the fleshy part of your palm.

Transfer the cooked fish to four serving plates. Each gets a few spoonfuls of warm chickpeas with two crisp panella alongside. Drizzle a high-quality olive oil over the fish and the chickpeas and finish with a sprinkling of crunchy sea salt and freshly ground black pepper.

PREPARATION NOTE

This dish calls for a fair amount of advance preparation. Both the chickpeas and the panella must be started the day before you are going to serve them.

Grilled
Mahimahi with Three-Bean Salad

We never had three-bean salad growing up, but as a chef who cooks seasonally, I use beans all summer long. This recipe makes a lot of Three Bean Salad—but that's okay, because it's even better the next day. In fact, it is better to make this recipe the day before you serve it—the salad, that is, not the fish. Grill the onion slices if you can. If not, sauté them in a pan with $\frac{1}{4}$ cup of olive oil, 1 teaspoon of salt, and $\frac{1}{2}$ teaspoon of pepper. Set aside to cool. **Serves 4**

**Four 6-ounce mahimahi steaks, about
    1³⁄₄ inches thick**

Extra-virgin olive oil

Sea salt

Freshly ground black pepper

Three-Bean Salad (recipe follows)

Prepare a charcoal fire and heat the grill over it.

Rub the fish on both sides with olive oil and season with salt and pepper. When the coals are white-hot, place the fish over the medium-high part of the fire (where you can hold your hand above the coals for, say, 4 seconds). If the flames jump to touch the fish, move them to a cooler part of the grill. Grill for 4 to 5 minutes per side, until the fish feel like the fleshy part of your palm.

Serve hot off the grill with the cold Three-Bean Salad alongside.

Three-Bean Salad Makes 7 cups

1 cup red-wine vinegar (preferably Chianti)

2 tablespoons dark brown sugar

1 large clove garlic, thinly sliced

2 cups extra-virgin olive oil

Sea salt

Freshly ground black pepper

2 cups Romano beans, stemmed and cut into 1-inch pieces

2 cups wax beans, stemmed and cut into 1-inch pieces

2 cups green beans or haricots verts, stemmed and cut into 1-inch pieces

½ cup oregano leaves

2 large red onions, thinly sliced and either grilled or sautéed (see headnote)

Bring a large pot of salted water to a boil for the beans.

In a small saucepan over a low flame, heat the vinegar, brown sugar, and garlic. Whisk together until the brown sugar completely dissolves. Transfer the mixture to a large mixing bowl. Add the olive oil in a slow, steady stream, whisking all the while. Add ½ teaspoon each salt and pepper.

When the bean water boils, begin adding the beans, group by group (they all have slightly different cooking times). As the Romano beans finish cooking—meaning when they are tender, say, 7 minutes—use a slotted spoon to transfer them to the mixing bowl with the dressing. Toss immediately. Add the wax beans to the boiling water. When they're tender, about 3 to 4 minutes, transfer them to the mixing bowl. Cook the green beans in the same way. When all of the beans have been cooked and are in the bowl, add the oregano and grilled onions. Toss thoroughly, cover with plastic wrap, and let sit for at least 1 hour or overnight. Taste before serving and if need be adjust the seasoning.

Grilled Shrimp
with Lemon-Thyme Vinaigrette and Hearts of Palm Salad

Key West shrimp are sweet and large, with pinkish white flesh. They come and go in my wholesale fish markets in New York City, but you can certainly substitute Gulf shrimp here. When you buy shrimp, have your fishmonger split the back and remove the gaga, the innards—it will save you the trouble of doing it yourself. Most shrimp are fairly bland, so the capers add some much needed tang. This dish can be served hot or at room temperature. However you serve it, make sure you have plenty of napkins: these shrimp are meant to be eaten with your fingers. I serve it with a fresh Hearts of Palm Salad to add just a touch of elegance to the meal. **Serves 4**

2 tablespoons red-wine vinegar (preferably Chianti)	**1½ pounds large shrimp, shells on, split down the back, vein removed**
2 tablespoons fresh lemon juice	**Freshly ground black pepper**
Sea salt	**1 tablespoon capers (preferably salt-packed)**
1 tablespoon thyme leaves, roughly chopped	**Hearts of Palm Salad (recipe follows)**
½ cup extra-virgin olive oil	

Prepare the vinaigrette by combining the vinegar, lemon juice, a pinch of salt, and the thyme. Whisk in the olive oil in a slow, steady stream.

Prepare a charcoal fire and heat the grill over it (or use a grill pan). Season the shrimp with salt and pepper. When the coals are white-hot, grill the shrimp until the shells are lightly charred and the shrimp are opaque, about 3 minutes per side. (It's always better to undercook than overcook!) Use tongs to transfer the cooked shrimp to a platter. Sprinkle with sea salt and freshly ground pepper.

Divide the shrimp among four plates. Sprinkle the capers on each plate and then drizzle each serving with some of the vinaigrette. Serve with the hearts of palm salad alongside.

Hearts of Palm Salad

Fresh hearts of palm have a completely different taste and texture than the canned ones we all grew up eating and hating. If you can't find fresh hearts of palm, don't substitute the canned or jarred variety. Use thinly sliced fresh artichokes instead. **Serves 4**

1 pound fresh hearts of palm
½ cup extra-virgin olive oil
⅓ cup fresh lemon juice

Leaves only of 2 sprigs thyme
Sea salt
Freshly ground black pepper

Using a mandolin or Benriner, slice the hearts of palm on the diagonal, creating paper-thin disks. In a medium mixing bowl, combine the hearts of palm with the olive oil, lemon juice, and thyme. Season with salt and pepper. Use your hands to toss thoroughly.

Pan-Fried & Sautéed

Wild Salmon
with Sea Beans

Wild (as opposed to farm-raised) salmon season typically runs from May 15 to September 15. These are fish that are getting ready to spawn in rivers from California to Alaska. Sea beans, also known as pousepied or sea asparagus, are green beans that grow in ocean bay beds. Their brininess cuts the fat in the salmon. Substitute green beans or pencil-thin asparagus if you can't find sea beans. **Serves 4**

1 small shallot, minced	**2 tablespoons chopped flat-leaf parsley**
2 tablespoons red-wine vinegar	**Four 6-ounce wild salmon fillets, skin on**
4 tablespoons extra-virgin olive oil	**Sea salt**
12 ounces green beans, stemmed	**Freshly ground black pepper**
2 ounces sea beans (see Sources, page 237)	**¼ cup canola oil**

In a medium bowl, combine the shallot, vinegar, and olive oil. Let sit for at least 3 hours or overnight.

Bring a large pot of salted water to a boil and cook the green beans until just tender, about 5 minutes. Drain in a colander and set aside to cool.

Whisk the shallot mixture to combine. Add the green beans, sea beans, and parsley, and toss to coat. Set aside.

Season the salmon fillets with salt and pepper. Heat the canola oil in a large, preferably nonstick, sauté pan over a medium-high flame until hot but not smoking. Place the fillets, skin side down, in the pan. Press the fillets down with your fingertips to give them full contact with the pan. Cook for about 5 minutes (the flesh side will appear cooked around the edges). Turn and continue to cook for just 1 more minute.

Transfer the salmon fillets to four serving plates. Serve with the reserved dressed beans alongside.

My Salmon
Eskimo Man

One day, out of the blue, the phone rang in the Esca kitchen. A voice I didn't recognize said without so much as a hello, "I have the best salmon you'll ever eat. Cooks Inlet king salmon." "Who's this?" I demanded. "My name's Frank. I'm an Eskimo calling from Alaska, but that's all you need to know. Whaddya got to lose? If the salmon's no good, just send it back. I'll pay for the shipping." A few days later, a box of the most beautiful salmon I've ever seen arrived at the restaurant.

Just looking at it, I knew it was going to be spectacular. It was dark, dark pink—a fantastic color for salmon. I ate a piece raw, and I knew that Frank was going to be selling me salmon for a long time. It really melted in my mouth. It was luxuriously fatty and rich-tasting. Sometimes Frank sent fish that still had roe in them. I always thought I was going to use the roe to create a special, but my cooks and I always ended up eating it ourselves.

I still don't know what Frank looks like. But I now know he lives in a fishing camp in a town of 150 people called Tyonek on Cook Inlet that's hours away from civilization. I looked it up on a map. The salmon swim from Cooks Inlet into the Susitna River to lay their eggs.

Frank doesn't even have a phone. I send my checks for the salmon to a guy named Lee who owns a laundromat fifty miles from Frank's house. One time Frank called and told me he shot three bears and a moose that he was going to freeze and eat in the winter. The guy eats seal. I bet Alaska seal is good. The water and land are incredibly clean, and the seals eat fish, so how bad could seal be? I've tried to get Frank to send me some seal, but he won't do it. If he ever did, I'd serve it at the restaurant. But for now my customers and I have to be content eating Eskimo Frank's amazing salmon.

Shad Roe with Dandelion Greens and Mustard Vinaigrette

To me, this dish is spring squared—shad roe and dandelion greens are quintessential spring ingredients. Shad roe must be cooked medium-rare, or it gets sawdusty, and the eggs get a little hard. When buying shad roe, look for orange eggs; if they're red, the eggs get gamy. Warning: Shad roe is not for everyone. Like I tell my waiters, "Don't oversell shad roe. If the customers know what it is, let them order it. If they don't know, let them find out about it somewhere else." **Serves 4**

2 tablespoons whole-grain mustard

2 tablespoons red-wine vinegar (preferably Chianti)

7 tablespoons extra-virgin olive oil

1 cup whole milk

1½ cups all-purpose flour

4 shad roe sacs

2 cups dandelion greens, rinsed well and spun-dry

Sea salt

Freshly ground black pepper

In a small mixing bowl, combine the mustard and vinegar. While still whisking, add 4 tablespoons of the olive oil in a slow, steady stream to form an emulsion. Set aside.

Heat the remaining 3 tablespoons olive oil in a large straight-sided sauté pan over a medium flame.

Pour the milk into a wide shallow bowl, and put the flour in a similar bowl. Coat the shad roe sacs with milk and then dredge in the flour, shaking off the excess. Transfer to the pan, and cook until golden brown, 4 to 5 minutes per side. Transfer to a paper-towel-lined plate.

Put the dandelion greens in a salad bowl. Whisk the vinaigrette again, pour over the greens, and toss to coat. Cut each piece of shad into ¼-inch slices. Divide the greens among four serving plates and top each serving with six slices of shad roe. Drizzle the dressing that remains in the salad bowl over the shad, top with a sprinkling of salt, and a grinding of pepper, and serve.

King Salmon
with Braised Fennel and Artichokes

This is one of salmon's greatest hits. The fennel adds just the right zingy touch. I call this my spring fling because the best artichokes come out of the ground in the spring and the best salmon are caught in the spring. King salmon is perhaps my favorite species: it's a big, buttery, sweet, fatty fish— all the things I like about salmon. To really taste how good king salmon is, cook it nice and slow skin side down. Braise the artichokes and fennel together. You'll see how well the flavors and textures marry. Don't use canned or jarred artichokes for this dish. **Serves 4**

Four 6-ounce wild salmon fillets, skin on

Sea salt

Freshly ground black pepper

3 tablespoons canola oil

3 tablespoons clarified butter (see Ingredient Note)

Braised Fennel and Artichokes (recipe follows)

Season the salmon fillets with salt and pepper. Heat the canola oil and clarified butter in a large, preferably nonstick, sauté pan over a medium-high flame until hot but not smoking. Place the fillets, skin side down, in the pan. Press the fillets down with your fingertips to give them full contact with the pan. Cook for about 5 minutes (the flesh side will appear cooked around the edges). Turn and continue to cook for just 1 more minute.

Transfer the salmon fillets to four serving plates and spoon the Braised Fennel and Artichokes alongside. Serve immediately.

INGREDIENT NOTE

Clarifying butter removes the milk solids, the part of butter that burns in the pan. To prepare it, melt a stick of butter over low heat and then let stand until it becomes solid again. Spoon off the white foamy top and discard. Store the clarified butter as you would regular butter and use the extra for the most golden brown grilled cheeses you've ever had.

Braised Fennel and Artichokes

The chiles really make the difference in this meltingly tender Braised Fennel, which goes well with virtually any fish dish that has no chiles or cayenne pepper. It's also good as a first course with some drizzled extra-virgin olive oil and a squeeze of lemon to finish the dish. **Serves 4**

½ cup extra-virgin olive oil

4 cloves garlic, thinly sliced

1 dried mild red chile
    (such as Italian finger hots or red Thai)

3 large fennel bulbs, cored, outer layers
    removed, and cut into matchsticks

4 large artichokes, outer leaves removed,
    head cut into thin slices

4 strips lemon peel

4 sprigs thyme

½ cup dry white wine

Sea salt

Freshly ground black pepper

Heat the olive oil in a large, straight-sided sauté pan over a medium-high flame until hot but not smoking. Add the garlic and the chile and cook until the garlic gives off its aroma, 2 to 3 minutes.

Add the fennel, artichokes, lemon peel, thyme, and wine to the pan. Stir well to combine. Bring to a simmer and cover the pot. Cook, stirring occasionally, until the fennel is meltingly tender, about 25 minutes. Check the liquid in the pan when stirring: the fennel should be half submerged. Add a little water if necessary.

When the fennel is tender, transfer the solids in the pan to a bowl using a slotted spoon. Raise the flame to high and reduce the pan liquid by half. Pour the liquid over the fennel, season with salt and pepper, and serve.

Tilefish
with Roasted Spring Vegetables

Tilefish is an East Coast fish that was thought to be extinct until it was discovered in the canyons of the North Atlantic when I was a teenager. It's also called golden spotted bass. The meat tastes like slightly watery crabmeat. This dish calls for sautéing the fish to get it nice and crispy and roasting the vegetables to lock in their flavor. **Serves 4**

FOR THE VEGETABLES

4 artichokes, outer leaves peeled, stems trimmed and quartered

1 medium parsnip, peeled

1 medium beet, peeled

1 small zucchini

¼ cup extra-virgin olive oil

1 teaspoon sea salt

1 teaspoon freshly ground black pepper

FOR THE TILEFISH

4 six-ounce tilefish fillets

3 tablespoons extra-virgin olive oil

1 cup Wondra (see Ingredient Note)

1 teaspoon sea salt, plus more to finish

1 teaspoon freshly ground black pepper, plus more to finish

MAKE THE VEGETABLES

Preheat the oven to 350°F.

Cut all of the vegetables into 3/4-inch chunks. Place them on a baking sheet and pour the olive oil over. Season with the salt and pepper, use your hands to toss, then spread the chunks into a single layer. Roast until all the vegetables are very tender when pierced with the tip of a knife, about 45 minutes. Transfer to a serving platter and serve hot or at room temperature.

MAKE THE FISH

Heat the olive oil in a large nonstick, sauté pan over a medium-high flame until hot but not smoking.

While the oil is heating, season the flour with the 1 teaspoon each of salt and pepper. Lightly dredge the fillets in the flour. Add the fillets to the pan and cook until lightly golden, about 4 minutes per side. Transfer the cooked fillets to a serving platter, and season with salt and pepper. Serve the fish and spring vegetables family- style.

INGREDIENT NOTE

I always use Wondra for frying fish. It's fine-milled into a soft, powdery flour so the excess is easily shaken off. It never clumps and it stands up to high heat, making for a cleanly fried piece of fish.

Black Bass with Three-Bean Salad

This is what I call a "Who doesn't like?" dish, as in who doesn't like black bass? And who doesn't like three-bean salad? Black bass is one of those fish I serve to avowed nonfish eaters, and Americans have been loving three-bean salad for hundreds of years. At least it seems that way. I bet even Thomas Jefferson ate three-bean salad.

Serves 4

3 tablespoons extra-virgin olive oil
Four 6-ounce black bass fillets, skin on
Sea salt

Freshly ground black pepper
1 cup Wondra (see Note, opposite)
Three-Bean Salad (page 129)

In a large sauté pan, heat the olive oil over a medium-high flame until just smoking.

Season the fillets with salt and pepper, and lightly dredge the skin side in the flour. Add the fillets to the pan, skin side down, and cook for 4 minutes, until the skin is crisp and brown. Turn and cook for just 1 or 2 minutes on the flesh side.

Transfer the fillets to four plates and serve with Three-Bean Salad alongside.

Black Bass

with Roasted Butternut Squash and Braised Purple Cabbage

If you cook seasonally on the East Coast, as I do, your options get limited in the late fall. This forces you to be creative with ingredients, as I am in this dish with the rose hips. If you can't find rose hips, use juniper berries. The roasted squash lends a lovely golden color that contrasts beautifully with the purple cabbage. I braise the cabbage to concentrate its flavor and to make it soft and tender. **Serves 4**

1 large or 2 small butternut squash, peeled and cut into 2-inch chunks
6 tablespoons extra-virgin olive oil
Sea salt
Freshly ground black pepper

Leaves of 2 sprigs sage
Four 6-ounce black bass fillets, skin on
1 cup Wondra (see Note, page 140)
Braised Purple Cabbage (recipe follows)

Preheat the oven to 350°F.

Spread the butternut squash on a baking sheet. Drizzle 3 tablespoons olive oil over, and season with 1 teaspoon salt and 1/2 teaspoon black pepper. Use your hands to toss; add the sage leaves and toss again. Bake until the squash are very tender, about 30 minutes.

When the squash has been in the oven for about 20 minutes, season the fillets with salt and pepper and lightly dredge the skin side in the flour. Heat the remaining 3 tablespoons oil in a large sauté pan over a medium-high flame until just smoking. Add the fillets to the pan, skin side down, and cook for 4 minutes, until the skin is crisp and brown. Turn and cook for just 1 or 2 more minutes on the flesh side. Transfer the fillets to four serving plates with the butternut squash and Braised Purple Cabbage alongside. Serve immediately.

Braised Purple Cabbage

Adding the pancetta and red-wine vinegar to purple cabbage makes this a soul-warming fall or winter dish. Serve it with any fish or pork or even a roast goose. **Serves 4**

1 large head purple cabbage	**2 cups apple cider**
3 tablespoons extra-virgin olive oil	**2 tablespoons brown sugar**
2 tablespoons rose hips or juniper berries	**Sea salt**
6 ounces pancetta, diced	**Freshly ground black pepper**
1 cup cipollini or pearl onions, peeled and diced	**1 bay leaf**
¾ cup red-wine vinegar (preferably Chianti)	

Peel off and discard the outer leaves of the cabbage. Then peel the remaining leaves until you get to the heart (which you will discard). Cut and discard the center rib from each leaf, then roll the leaves like a cigar. Cut the rolled leaves into ¹/₂-inch ribbons.

Heat the olive oil over a medium flame in a heavy-bottomed pot with a tight-fitting lid. When it's hot but not smoking, add the rose hips or juniper berries and infuse the oil for a minute. Add the diced pancetta and cook until lightly browned and crisp. Add the cipollini and sauté until they begin to caramelize, about 5 minutes.

Add the vinegar, cider, and brown sugar, and bring to a boil. Add the cabbage, and season with 1/2 teaspoon salt, several turns of a pepper mill, and the bay leaf. Stir thoroughly to coat the cabbage with the fat and liquid. Lower the flame to simmer, cover, and cook, stirring occasionally, until the cabbage is very tender, about 40 minutes. The mixture should be moist but not wet; if the pan begins to dry out, add a bit of water. Remove and discard the bay leaf. Season with salt and pepper before serving.

Trout
Almost Amandine
with Pistachios

This is my take on trout amandine, made
with pistachios instead. Italians love
pistachios, so this dish goes hand in hand with my love of everything
Italian. I toast the pistachios and crush them, "bread" the trout in them,
lay lemon slices on top of the fish, and throw the whole thing under the
broiler. Any trout will do for this dish, but I use golden trout whenever I can
get my hands on some, because I love the color of the flesh. **Serves 4**

3 tablespoons unsalted butter, melted
3 tablespoons extra-virgin olive oil
½ cup pistachios, shelled and crushed
Four 6-ounce boneless trout fillets

Sea salt
Freshly ground black pepper
2 lemons, sliced ¼-inch thick

Preheat the broiler.

Combine the butter and olive oil in a wide shallow bowl. Place the crushed
pistachios in another wide shallow bowl.

Season the trout fillets with salt and pepper. Slide the fillets through the butter-
oil mixture, then press the flesh side down into the pistachios. Place the fillets, skin
side down, on a baking sheet, and top each with two or three lemon slices.

Broil the fish for 6 to 8 minutes, until the nuts are golden brown and the fish has
begun to flake. Serve immediately, with the bubbling butter and oil spooned over.

Swordfish
with Broccoli Rabe

There are few fish in the sea that fight as hard as a swordfish. I've never caught one, although God knows I've tried. A lot of people have misconceptions about swordfish. First of all, though swordfish were overfished a few years ago, that problem has now been rectified, and now there are plenty of swordfish in the sea. Second, swordfish should be rosy, not pale white; the rosiness is a sign of quality and freshness. Searing the swordfish gets it nice and crusty and seals in the juices and flavor. And the bitterness of the broccoli rabe plays beautifully off the meaty sweetness of the swordfish. **Serves 4**

7 tablespoons extra-virgin olive oil, plus high-quality extra-virgin olive oil, for drizzling

6 large cloves garlic, crushed with the blade of a knife

2 dried mild red chiles (such as Italian finger hots)

2 bunches broccoli rabe, very thick stem ends removed and discarded, stalks cut into 2-inch pieces

Juice of 1 lemon

1 teaspoon sea salt

1/2 teaspoon freshly ground black pepper

Four 6-ounce swordfish steaks, about 1 1/2 inches thick

In a large, preferably nonstick, skillet with a tight-fitting lid, heat 4 tablespoons of the olive oil over a medium flame until hot but not smoking. Add the garlic and chiles and stir until their aromas are released, about 2 minutes. Add the lower stems of the broccoli rabe, stir to coat with the oil, then cover. Cook for 10 to 12 minutes, stirring occasionally, until the stems are tender. Add the stalk pieces and the florets, replace the lid, and cook for 6 to 8 minutes more. Add the lemon juice, salt, and pepper. Set aside and keep warm.

    Add the remaining 3 tablespoons olive oil to the hot pan over a medium-high flame. Place the swordfish steaks in the pan, and cook for 4 to 6 minutes per side; the fish should yield but not break when you touch your finger to it. Transfer the steaks to four serving plates and serve immediately with the broccoli rabe alongside.

Monkfish with Sautéed Wild Mushrooms and Chestnuts

This is one of my fall mainstays, because all three main ingredients are abundant as the leaves change. Monkfish is known as the poor man's lobster, but that's because of the texture and color and not the flavor, which is nowhere as sweet as lobster. Don't be put off if you see a whole monkfish in a fish store because it's one ugly fish. It looks like some kind of seagoing monster. **Serves 4**

8 large or 10 medium chestnuts
Sautéed Wild Mushrooms (page 207)
Four 6-ounce monkfish tails

Sea salt
Freshly ground black pepper
3 tablespoons canola oil

Preheat the oven to 350°F.

Using a paring knife, score the chestnuts with an X. Roast the nuts in the preheated oven for about 20 minutes, until you see the shells beginning to separate from the meat. Remove from the oven and when they are cool enough to handle, peel and discard the shells.

Put the Sautéed Wild Mushrooms into a large sauté pan, add the chestnuts, stir to combine, and keep warm over a very low flame. Taste to adjust the seasoning.

Season the monkfish with salt and pepper. Heat the canola oil in a large, preferably nonstick, pan until almost smoking. Place the monkfish in the pan—it should sizzle—and cook until golden brown, about 3 minutes per side.

Serve the monkfish on four plates, with the chestnuts and mushrooms alongside.

Roasted, Baked, & Poached

Whole Mediterranean Fish
with Caperberries and Green Olives

Mediterranean fish have great taste, and species like sea bream and branzino are now readily available in fish markets around the country. Roasting olives intensifies their flavor, and the olives combined with the capers give this dish real depth. Caperberries are a little meatier than regular capers; make sure they have been preserved in brine rather than vinegar. I knew this dish was a winner when William Grimes raved about it in *The New York Times*. *Note:* The recipe serves two people. **Serves 2**

½ pound Sicilian olives

½ cup caperberries

1 whole fish (about 3 to 4 pounds), such as sea bream, branzino, or dorado, scaled and cleaned

4 sprigs rosemary

3 sprigs parsley

3 cloves garlic, thinly sliced

2 lemons, thinly sliced

Sea salt

Freshly ground black pepper

¼ cup extra-virgin olive oil

¼ cup dry white wine

Preheat the oven to 450°F.

In a small bowl, combine the olives and caperberries, and toss to combine. Set aside.

Stuff the cavity of the fish with the rosemary, parsley, garlic, and a few lemon slices. Season the fish with salt and pepper.

Place the fish in an oval enamel roasting pan and surround with the caperberries and olives. Drizzle the olive oil and wine over the fish and cover with the remaining lemon slices. Roast for about 30 minutes, until the skin is crispy and the fish feels tender.

Put a trivet on the table and serve the fish in the pan. Use a spoon to break the flesh away along the top side (where it will have begun to pull away from the bone). Slide the spoon under each fillet but over the spine, and lift the fillet onto a plate. Turn the fillet over, spoon some olives and caperberries over it, along with the wine that the fish was cooked in. Repeat with the other fillet.

The Special of the Day (and Night)

When the call comes that the fish are biting, day or night, winter or summer, you have to go. Such a call came one frigid night in late December. I was still in the restaurant at 10:00 P.M., prepping some porgies for the next day's menu. It was Captain Joe; he'd been tipped off to a sea bass spot where the fish were so plentiful you could practically pick them out of the water with your hands. That is, if you didn't mind plunging your hands into 50° ocean water. "Meet me at the docks at 1 A.M. Tell Donna I'll have you home by three in the afternoon."

After we had served 225 dinners that night I caught the 10:54 train out of Penn Station. I was home by midnight, changed into winter fishing clothes—long johns, wool socks, a fleece-lined Gore-Tex top, dungarees, rubber fishing pants, knit cap, commercial fishing boots, and a good turtleneck.

I showed up at the dock at 1 A.M., to be greeted by a grunt from Captain Joe. Joe is in his sixties, and one look at his weathered face lets you know he's spent the better part of his life fishing on the ocean. Emil, Joe's son-in-law, and Joe's ten-year-old grandson Mike were also along for the ride. So was John Simonelli—Simo, we call him. Simo is out of his friggin' mind, works in air freight at Kennedy Airport. He's a charismatic, gnarled, tattooed old biker.

Joe ran the boat until we got out of the inlet, about an hour, then Emil took over the wheel while Joe slept. I kept Emil company to be a lookout because you really couldn't see anything in the pitch black that surrounded us. Joe had had two boats that sank when he ran into large floating objects in the middle of the night.

We made it to the spot in three hours, by 4:30 A.M. Emil slowed the engines down, so I knew it was close to fishing time. Joe was up in the wheelhouse with his little piece of paper. I asked him exactly where we were, but I knew he'd never tell me. Joe protects his sources and his spots. Usually he gives you half of the coordinates, some spot that was actually a mile away from where the fish were. He's got coordinates scribbled all over the boat's dashboard, a bizarre form of fisherman's graffiti. A couple of years ago Joe watched his boat sink and still managed to write down the coordinates as he was rescued by a passing boat.

We put a couple of rods down with 12-ounce sinkers using shucked chowder clams as bait. The water is 234 feet deep, so I always tell people you're never more than a twenty-fifth of a mile from land out here, it's just that the land is covered in water. Lots of water. There's a good deal of cranking involved to get your line down that far. Joe uses an electric reel, but I use an old-fashioned manual jobbie, so it takes a while longer for me to get my line down. But as soon as my line was all the way down, the fish, mostly sea bass, were biting like crazy. If there were three hooks on your rod, you caught three fish in seconds. We couldn't pull in the fish fast enough.

We caught 70 pounds of pollack, some lingcod (whiting), and 617 pounds of sea bass. One of the sea bass I caught had just eaten some scungilli, so when I unhooked it the fish spit it out. I then used that scungilli as bait to catch the one lousy cod we caught, a twenty pounder. Everybody else was a little annoyed when I caught the only cod, because that was the whole point of the fishing trip. Cod is king.

Joe said we were going to be back by three in the afternoon. But at 3 P.M. we were still 70 miles offshore. Hey, when the fish are biting you don't leave. Joe always wants to stay out. Joe's nickname is Captain Midnight. His tombstone is going to read, "One More Drift." Emil said we gotta get home for his kid. Mikey was looking a little cold, a little green at the gills, so we headed home. We did hit one last spot at 6 P.M., but we didn't stay there long.

We all froze our tootsies off on the way home. Once the sun goes down it gets really cold on the ocean in late December. You're going sixteen knots, the wind is kicking in your face, and there's no heat on the boat. We arrived at the dock at 11 P.M. We had been on Joe's boat for twenty-two cold, wet, and windy hours. And yet all I kept thinking was what a great day of fishing it had been. You don't get many days like that in your life. Everyone was exhausted, their teeth chattering, but they were thrilled. We cleaned the boat on the way in, unloaded the catch, iced down the fish, and headed home. Donna gave me a look as I walked in the door, but she knows me well enough to know that when the fish are biting, all bets are off. Even when it's freezing cold in late December.

I brought the twenty-pound cod to the restaurant the next night, filleted and roasted it with olives and artichokes, and served it. I told the waitstaff to tell our customers that the cod was the special of the day and night.

Cod with Spaghetti Squash and Oven-Dried Tomatoes

My mother used to bake spaghetti squash, put it in tomato sauce, and toss it with pasta. This dish is sort of a seafood version of that. Oven-drying tomatoes is the best way to make something delicious out of the cardboardlike Roma tomatoes we in the Northeast have to cook with all winter, concentrating their flavor. The tomatoes take about 3 hours in the oven; they can be prepared ahead and stored, covered in olive oil, at room temperature. Halibut would make a fine substitute for the cod if you wanted to gussy up this dish a bit. **Serves 4**

1 large spaghetti squash (about 2½ pounds)

3 tablespoons extra-virgin olive oil, plus high-quality extra-virgin olive oil, for drizzling

Sea salt

Freshly ground black pepper

Four 6-ounce cod fillets, about 1¾ inches thick

Oven-Dried Tomatoes (page 205)

Preheat the oven to 400°F. Line a baking sheet with parchment paper or aluminum foil.

Halve the squash lengthwise, through the stem, and scoop out the seeds. Drizzle the flesh side with olive oil, spreading it with your fingers to completely coat the squash, and season with salt and pepper. Place the squash, cut side down, on the prepared baking sheet. Bake until completely soft when pierced with a fork, 45 to 50 minutes.

Remove the squash from the oven, reduce the oven temperature to 350°F, and, when it is cool enough to handle, scoop out the flesh. Spread the cooked squash on the bottom of a 9 x 9-inch baking dish.

Season the fish with salt and pepper on both sides and arrange on top of the squash. Top each fillet with two tomato halves (from the Oven-Dried Tomatoes) and bake until the fish is just cooked through, about 15 minutes. The fish should feel like it will almost break apart when you touch it.

Use a spatula to transfer portions of the spaghetti squash and cod to serving plates. Drizzle with high-quality extra-virgin olive oil and serve immediately.

Cod with Polenta and Sautéed Wild Mushrooms

This is a soul-warming preparation that helps stave off the winter blahs. The cod is sweet and buttery, the earthy mushrooms ground the dish, and the polenta adds just the right creamy touch. I use Anson Mills' stone-ground polenta (see Sources, page 237) because it cooks up beautifully. I love to have a plate of this merluzzo when I've shoveled my driveway after a snowstorm or when I've come back from a winter fishing expedition. **Serves 4**

3 tablespoons extra-virgin olive oil, plus high-quality extra-virgin olive oil, for drizzling

1 cup Wondra (see Note, page 140)

Sea salt

Freshly ground black pepper

Four 6-ounce skinless cod fillets, about 1¾ inches thick

1½ cups Anson Mills stone-ground polenta, prepared according to package directions, kept warm (see Preparation Note)

Sautéed Wild Mushrooms (page 207), assorted types

Aceto balsamico (aged balsamic vinegar), for drizzling

Preheat the oven to 400°F.

Heat 3 tablespoons of the olive oil in a large, nonstick sauté pan with an ovenproof handle over a medium-high flame until hot but not smoking.

Season the flour with 1 teaspoon each of salt and pepper. Lightly dredge the cod fillets in the seasoned flour, then place the fillets in the hot pan (they should sizzle). Cook for about 3 minutes per side to get a nice golden brown coating. Transfer the pan to the oven. Cook for 4 minutes, until the fish is cooked through but not dry; the fillets should feel firm but not tight. Remove from the heat and season with a drizzling of sea salt and a few turns of a pepper grinder.

Spoon a few tablespoons of the warm polenta onto the center of each of four serving plates. Top with the cod and the Sautéed Wild Mushrooms. Finish with a drizzle of high-quality olive oil and *aceto balsamico* around the plate.

PREPARATION NOTE

Keep the polenta warm in a bain-marie (water bath) with pats of butter and freshly ground black pepper on top while the rest of the dish is prepared. Finish this dish with a drizzle of *aceto balsamico* (aged balsamic vinegar), the good stuff.

"**COD** is the most important fish in the world, historically and commercially, and **I LOVE THE STUFF.** It was my grandmother's favorite fish. Her name was Gertie Pasternack, and she had a little family-style restaurant in Coney Island, and she never, ever ate fish off the bone (a fillet). She would heat the cod over a low flame, without liquid, so it would sort of braise itself."

Slow-Roasted Black Cod

Inspired by the bagels-and-lox brunches my parents served, I came up with this wonderful winter preparation. Black cod, also known as sable, is an increasingly popular West Coast fish that my friend Nobu Matsuhisa has made famous. It's a fairly oily fish, so I cook it slowly to get rid of some of the fat. The horseradish helps cut the richness, as does the fennel. **Serves 4**

3/4 pound fingerling potatoes (about 12)

1/3 cup finely grated horseradish

1/2 cup plus 3 tablespoons extra-virgin olive oil

2 tablespoons plus 2 teaspoons lemon juice

Sea salt

1 large fennel bulb, halved, cored, outer layer removed, and sliced into matchsticks

2 bay leaves

2 sprigs thyme

Freshly ground black pepper

Four 6-ounce black cod fillets, about 1 3/4 inches thick, skin on

Preheat the oven to 250°F.

Place the potatoes in a large saucepan of salted water and bring to a boil. Cook the potatoes for about 10 minutes, until soft when pierced with a paring knife but still firm enough to keep their shape. Drain. When cool enough to handle, remove the skins and cut each in half; set aside.

Meanwhile, in a small bowl, combine the horseradish, 1/2 cup olive oil, 2 tablespoons lemon juice, and 1/4 teaspoon sea salt. Blend with a fork. Set aside.

Place the fennel, bay leaves, thyme, and 1 teaspoon lemon juice in a large, straight-sided sauté pan. Add just enough water to cover and season with a sprinkling of salt and a few grindings of pepper. Bring to a boil over a high flame, reduce the heat to low, and cover. Cook until the fennel is just barely tender, about 10 minutes. Add the potatoes and the remaining 1 teaspoon lemon juice and continue to cook until the fennel and potatoes are soft and the pan is almost dry, about 5 minutes.

Dry the fish with paper towels, then season with salt and pepper. In a large, preferably nonstick, sauté pan with an ovenproof handle, heat the remaining 3 tablespoons olive oil over a high flame. Place the fish in the pan, skin side down, and cook until the skin is seared, 3 to 4 minutes. Transfer to the oven and slow-roast for 12 to 14 minutes, until the fish begins to flake when you touch it.

Spoon equal portions of the fennel-potato mixture onto each of four plates. Top each serving with a fillet and a small dollop of the reserved freshly grated horseradish.

Left and above: Salt-Baked *Pesce per Due* (page 160)

Salt-Baked
Pesce per Due

To me there's nothing sexier than serving your honey an elegantly prepared and presented whole fish for two. Make a show of deftly removing the bones, and you'll win her heart forever. The fish shouldn't be too big—figure 2 pounds for two people. And just pop it into the oven with lemon and some olives. In this preparation the olives are transformed into another soft and sexy food. I like to use firm olives here, like the Sicilian greens (Cerignolas), but you can really use whatever olives you have on hand. Some earthy braised greens complement the fish. **Serves 2**

One 2-pound fish (such as branzino, dorado, or black sea bass)

3¹/₂ cups fine sea salt

3 large egg whites

4 sprigs flat-leaf parsley, stems and leaves separated, leaves chopped, for garnish

2 sprigs rosemary

4 Sicilian olives

1 clove garlic

2 slices lemon

Braised Greens (recipe follows)

Preheat the oven to 400°F.

Trace a rough outline of the whole fish on a piece of parchment paper, and cut it out.

In a mixing bowl, combine 3 cups of the salt and the egg whites with a wooden spoon (the mixture should feel like wet sand).

Place the parsley stems, rosemary, olives, garlic, and lemon slices in the cavity of the fish. Spread the remaining ¹/₂ cup salt over a baking tray. Place the cut-out parchment paper on the salt and place the fish on top. Use your hands to cover the whole fish with the salt-and-egg-white mixture, pressing down onto the fish to pack it tightly. Bake for 18 to 20 minutes, without turning, until the salt crust is hard and golden brown.

Bring the baking tray to the table. Crack the salt crust with the handle of a knife and peel it away. Use a spoon to break the flesh away along the top side (where it will have begun to pull away from the bone). Slide the spoon under the fillet but over the spine, and lift the fillet onto a dinner plate. Turn the fish over and plate the other fillet. Garnish the fish with the chopped parsley and serve with Braised Greens alongside.

Photographs on pages 158–59

Braised Greens

These greens prove once again that everything goes better with bacon. Hey, sometimes you need a side order of pork to get your iron intake. **Serves 4**

6 ounces pancetta, cut into ¹⁄₂-inch lardoons

¹⁄₄ cup extra-virgin olive oil

2 cloves garlic, thinly sliced

4 bunches assorted greens
  (broccoli rabe, escarole, Swiss chard, kale),
  rinsed, spun dry, and stemmed

¹⁄₂ teaspoon sea salt

Freshly ground black pepper

2 tablespoons high-quality extra-virgin olive oil,
  to finish

In a straight-sided sauté pan with a tight-fitting lid, cook the pancetta over a medium flame until browned, about 4 minutes. Spoon all but 2 tablespoons of fat out of the pan, then add the ¹⁄₄ cup olive oil and garlic to the pancetta. Cook until the garlic is softened, about 3 minutes. Add the greens and use tongs to toss, coating them with the olive oil and shrinking their volume significantly. Season with the salt and some freshly ground pepper.

Add about ¹⁄₄ cup water to the pan, then cover. Cook the greens until tender, about 20 minutes. Stir frequently and add a bit more water as necessary—there should always be about ¹⁄₂ inch liquid in the bottom of the pan. As the greens become tender, remove the lid and let the liquid evaporate so the greens are moist but not wet. With a slotted spoon, transfer the cooked greens to a serving bowl and toss with the 2 tablespoons high-quality extra-virgin olive oil. Serve immediately.

Baked Bluefish
with Stewed Oyster Mushrooms

It's a funny thing about bluefish: most people shy away from it just the way they do from mackerel because they think it's too oily, funky, and fishy. But a freshly caught bluefish that's been handled properly is a great eating fish. So the key is buying the right one: a whole fish, one that's bright and firm and no bigger than 3½ pounds, a relatively small snapper blue that's been properly handled and has a very thin blood line, that dark line up the middle of the fish that has turned off generations of fish lovers. Have your fishmonger fillet it in front of you. The stewed oyster mushrooms stand up well to the bluefish. **Serves 4**

3 vine-ripened tomatoes, sliced ¼ inch thick

Sea salt

4 yellow onions, cut into ¼-inch slices

2 tablespoons extra-virgin olive oil, plus more for drizzling

Freshly ground black pepper

1 clove garlic, thinly sliced

2½ cups Italian-Style Bread Crumbs (page 233; omit the lemon zest)

½ cup basil leaves

½ cup flat-leaf parsley leaves

Four 8-ounce bluefish fillets, skin on

1½ cups Clam or Lobster Stock (page 75)

Stewed Oyster Mushrooms (recipe follows)

Preheat the oven to 350°F.

Lay the tomato slices on a baking sheet and sprinkle with about 1/2 teaspoon of salt to draw some of their liquid out. Set aside for 1 hour.

Meanwhile, place the onion slices on another baking sheet, drizzle generously with olive oil, season with salt and pepper, and toss to coat. Roast the onions until very tender, about 15 minutes.

Heat the 2 tablespoons olive oil in a small sauté pan over a medium flame. Add the garlic and sauté until just golden, about 4 minutes. (If the garlic begins to burn and embitters the oil, start again.) Remove and discard the garlic with a slotted spoon and reserve the oil. Set aside. Leave the oven on.

In the workbowl of a food processor, combine the bread crumbs with the basil and parsley leaves. Pulse until the mixture is green from the herbs and fully combined.

Arrange the bluefish fillets in the center of a Pyrex or enameled baking dish and spread the reserved tomato slices over the fish. Spread the roasted onions around the fillets and then cover everything with a sprinkling of the bread crumb mixture. Pour the Clam or Lobster Stock around the fish and onions, then drizzle the garlic-infused oil over the top.

Bake the fish until the bread crumbs are golden on top, about 12 minutes. Set the bubbling baking dish on a trivet for family-style service. Serve the mushrooms on the side.

Stewed Oyster Mushrooms Serves 4

6 ounces pancetta, cut into small dice

1 pint cipollini or pearl onions, peeled

½ cup red-wine vinegar (preferably Chianti)

One 16½-ounce can San Marzano tomatoes, with their juice

1 bay leaf

1 teaspoon sea salt

½ teaspoon freshly ground black pepper

Sautéed Wild Mushrooms (page 207), made with 1 pound oyster mushrooms

Trace a circle of parchment paper the same diameter as a large, straight-sided sauté pan. Cut it out and set aside.

Place the diced pancetta in the sauté pan over a medium-high flame. Sauté the pancetta until it browns and renders its fat, about 4 minutes. Drain all but 2 tablespoons of fat from the pan. Add the onions, stirring occasionally, and cook until they start to take on color, about 7 minutes. Add the vinegar to deglaze the pan, and stir for 2 to 3 minutes. By now the onions should be tender.

Add the tomatoes and bay leaf and stir. Season with the salt and pepper. Break up the tomatoes with a fork, and simmer for about 15 minutes. Add the sautéed mushrooms. Place the parchment paper on top of the stewing mushrooms, cover with a lid, and turn down the heat to a simmer. Cook until the mushrooms are tender, about 30 to 45 minutes. Discard the bay leaf and serve.

Pan-Roasted Cod
with Spinach and Clementines

In the winter in New York City, you have to be a little more creative because you have less to work with. Clementines are one of my great winter pleasures. They're readily available and easy to cook with because they have no pits. They do break down easily, so I always put them into the roasting pan during the last minute of cooking. The spinach adds some body to the dish. **Serves 4**

4 clementines or tangerines
Four 6-ounce cod fillets, about 1¾ inches thick
Sea salt
Freshly ground black pepper
¼ cup extra-virgin olive oil

1 cup Wondra (see Note, page 140)
3 bunches spinach, cleaned and stemmed
Pressed tangerine oil or high-quality extra-virgin olive oil, for drizzling

Preheat the oven to 400°F.

Zest the clementines (you'll need both the zest and the flesh for the recipe); use a chef's knife to slice the top and bottom off the clementines so that they stand flat on a cutting board. Cut the peel away from the flesh in wide strips from top to bottom. Cut each segment away from the membrane.

Dry the fillets with paper towels, then season them with salt and pepper. In a large ovenproof sauté pan, heat 3 tablespoons of the olive oil over a high flame until it's hot but not smoking. Lightly dredge the skin side of the fillets in the flour. Place the fillets in the pan, skin side down, and cook for about 3 minutes, until browned. Turn and sear the other side for 3 to 4 minutes, until well browned. Transfer to the oven to finish cooking for 3 to 4 minutes, or until the fillets begin to flake when you press them with your finger.

While the cod is in the oven, heat the remaining 1 tablespoon olive oil in a sauté pan over a medium flame. Add the clementine zests and stir for about 1 minute, until aromatic. Add the spinach, season with salt and pepper, and use tongs to toss occasionally until tender, about 4 minutes. Add the clementine segments for the last minute of cooking. Remove from the heat.

Serve the cod fillets on a bed of spinach with the clementine segments placed around them. Drizzle with pressed tangerine oil or a high-quality extra-virgin olive oil. Don't forget a sprinkle of salt and pepper.

Baked Bluefish
with Morels and Asparagus

This is a cheap fish (bluefish) married to a luxury item (morels), so the two together balance out the overall cost of the dish. Bluefish and morels are a great combination, because the morels can stand up to the bluefish's pronounced flavor. You really shouldn't substitute cultivated mushrooms for the morels. Button mushrooms can't withstand the flavor onslaught that is bluefish. Turn to page 237 for sources for morels.

This dish uses the small snapper blues. Red snapper fillets can be substituted when blues aren't running. **Serves 4**

1 pound morel mushrooms

1 bunch jumbo asparagus, cut on the bias
    into 1-inch pieces, tips left intact

1/4 pound plus 2 tablespoons butter

2 shallots, minced

1/4 cup brandy

Sea salt

Freshly ground black pepper

Four 8-ounce bluefish fillets, skin on

Extra-virgin olive oil, plus high-quality
    extra-virgin olive oil for drizzling

1/2 cup Italian-Style Bread Crumbs (page 233)

Clean the morels in 3 changes of clean water; submerge them in a bowl of water, move them gently with your fingers, and let them sit, giving the sand a chance to settle. Remove the morels, empty and rinse the bowl, and repeat the process 2 more times. Gently pat them dry with paper towels.

Preheat the oven to 450°F.

Bring a large pot of salted water to a boil. Add the asparagus and blanch for 3 minutes. Drain in a colander and set aside.

Melt the 1/4 pound butter in a large, straight-sided sauté pan. When the foam subsides, add the shallots and cook until translucent, about 3 minutes. Add the morels and cook, stirring frequently, until the mushrooms begin to soften, 3 to 5 minutes.

Remove the pan from the heat and add the brandy (it will flame if you add it over the heat). Return it to the heat, bring the liquid to a strong simmer, and cook for 3 minutes to cook off the alcohol. Season the mushrooms with salt and pepper; then cover with either a circle of parchment paper pressed gently to the surface of the mushrooms or a tight-fitting lid. Cook over a medium-low flame for 10 to 12 minutes, until the morels are tender.

continued

Add the asparagus to the pan, stir to combine, and bring to a simmer, then remove from the heat.

Pour the contents of the pan into a 12-inch oval enamel baking dish. Spread the mixture to cover the bottom.

Brush the skin side of the fillets with olive oil and place them, skin side up, in the baking dish on top of the morel mixture. Sprinkle the dish with the bread crumbs, concentrating mostly on the edges of the dish. Drizzle the fish with extra-virgin olive oil, a few small pieces of butter, a sprinkling of sea salt.

Bake the fish for 5 to 7 minutes and then finish in a hot broiler for 2 minutes. The casserole should be lightly golden and bubbling hot.

Whole Turbot with
Meyer Lemon and Blood Orange

This is a nifty and elegant dish for two. Turbot is a magnificent (if very expensive), rich-tasting fish, but it's the presentation here that makes the dish special: I slice the blood oranges and Meyer lemons, macerate them with a few chopped basil leaves, and spoon that mixture over the turbot. Beautiful. **Serves 2**

2 Meyer lemons, thinly sliced

1 blood orange, thinly sliced

3 sprigs basil, leaves chopped, stems reserved

$^1/_2$ cup plus 2 tablespoons extra-virgin olive oil, plus high-quality extra-virgin olive oil, for drizzling

Sea salt

Freshly ground black pepper

One 2-pound turbot

In a small bowl, combine the lemon and orange slices, basil leaves, $^1/_2$ cup of olive oil, and $^1/_2$ teaspoon each salt and pepper. Toss gently to combine, and set aside for 1 hour.

Preheat the oven to 450°F.

Season both sides of the fish with salt and pepper and rub with the remaining 2 tablespoons olive oil. Put the reserved basil stems into the cavity and place the fish on a baking sheet. Bake for 18 to 20 minutes, until the fish feels like it's flaking when you press it with your finger.

Use a spoon to break the flesh away along the top side (where it will have begun to pull away from the bone). Slide the spoon under the fillet but over the spine, and lift the fillet onto a serving plate. Turn the fish over and serve the other fillet. Spoon the lemon-orange mixture over the top and drizzle with high-quality extra-virgin olive oil.

Pan-Roasted Cobia with Zucchini and Olives

I admit it: I came up with this dish because I needed to get rid of some zucchini. Whenever one of my farmers offers me zucchini, I make him give it to me free. Paying for something that ubiquitous in season doesn't make sense. Zucchini and olives are a fine combination: the strong flavor of the olives marries well with the zucchini's grassiness. I use Calabrese olives—small green olives brined with red pepper and wild fennel. Between the wild fennel and the garlic and rosemary, this dish smells great. It's aromatic as hell. It would make a great men's cologne. Any summer squash works well with the recipe. **Serves 4**

1½ pounds early-summer squashes (pattypan, eight ball, zucchini, whatever), cut into 2-inch pieces

¼ cup extra-virgin olive oil, plus high-quality extra-virgin olive oil, for drizzling

Sea salt

Freshly ground black pepper

¼ pound assorted pitted olives (Calabrese, Sicilian, Alfonse), roughly chopped

¼ cup chopped fresh mint leaves

¼ cup canola oil

Four 6-ounce cobia fillets, 1¾ inches thick

Preheat the oven to 400°F.

Cut all the zucchini in half lengthwise, and then cut into ½-inch slices and spread on a baking sheet. Toss with the ¼ cup olive oil and season with salt and pepper. Roast for 10 minutes. Add the olives and continue cooking about 20 minutes more, until the zucchini are tender and the olives have shrunken and cracked. Remove from the oven. Add the mint leaves and toss. Set aside.

Season the fillets on both sides with salt and pepper.

In a large cast-iron pan, heat the canola oil over a medium flame until just smoking. Sear the fish for 3 or 4 minutes, turn, and cook until the fish is opaque, 3 or 4 minutes more. Serve with the roasted zucchini alongside and drizzle high-quality extra-virgin olive oil over the top.

Turbot in Cortocio with Apple and Cinzano

Most people think of turbot as French, but they eat it all the time in Italy as well. It's a flat fish with a distinctive, rich flavor. *Cortocio* is a method of baking fish in parchment paper, and it couldn't be easier or yield better results. The fish stays really moist, and when you bring the parchment to the table and tear it open, it's like a great dramatic moment in a play: the crowd will definitely ooh and aah. The Cinzano brings a touch of dryness and the apple brings sweetness and crunch. Don't use a tart apple variety, such as a Granny Smith, here; the dish needs the sweetness a Gala or Honeycrisp supplies. This is an expensive preparation; use black sea bass instead of turbot to save money. **Serves 4**

3½ tablespoons unsalted butter

1 Gala or Honeycrisp apple,
    peeled and cut into a medium dice

7 tablespoons extra-virgin olive oil

½ pound black trumpet mushrooms, cleaned

1 tablespoon chopped tarragon

1 tablespoon chopped flat-leaf parsley

1 teaspoon chopped chives

2 large eggs, lightly beaten

Four 6-ounce turbot fillets

Sea salt

Freshly ground black pepper

2 tablespoons apple cider

2 tablespoons Cinzano or dry vermouth

Preheat the oven to 450°F.

Melt 1½ tablespoons of the butter in a small sauté pan. Add the diced apple. Stirring frequently, cook until the apple is lightly caramelized, about 4 minutes. Transfer the apple to a small bowl and set aside.

Add 3 tablespoons of the olive oil to the pan and heat over a medium-high flame. Add the mushrooms and sauté, stirring frequently, for about 6 minutes, until well browned. Set aside.

In a small bowl, combine the tarragon, parsley, and chives. Set aside.

Cut four parchment paper squares, each about 20 x 15 inches. Fold the squares in half to make a crease. Brush the edges with the beaten egg. Drizzle about 1 tablespoon olive oil in the center of each square and use your fingers to spread the oil over the paper.

Place the fish fillets on the lower half of each paper square and season with salt and pepper. Top each fillet with 1 teaspoon each of the reserved apple and mushrooms. Sprinkle the reserved herb mixture equally over the tops and finish each fillet with 1/2 tablespoon butter.

Drizzle 1 teaspoon each apple cider and Cinzano over each fillet, then fold the paper squares over so the edges meet. Fold the corners in first and then fold the edges in all around, sealing them by twisting the corners. Brush the parchment packets with the remaining beaten egg and place them on a baking sheet. Bake the packets for 6 to 8 minutes, until the paper has puffed up and turned golden. Transfer the packets to serving plates, and use the tip of a paring knife to open them.

Striped Bass
with Sweet Potatoes and Sautéed Wild Mushrooms

Most people wouldn't think of roasting sweet potatoes to serve with their fish, but the sweetness of the potatoes goes really well with the earthiness of the mushrooms; portobellos work great here; and wild mushrooms would take this dish to a new level of deliciousness. If it's not striped bass season, use tuna, salmon, or cod instead. **Serves 4**

**5 medium sweet potatoes,
    peeled and cut into 2-inch chunks**

**¼ cup extra-virgin olive oil, plus high-quality
    extra-virgin olive oil, for drizzling**

Sea salt

Freshly ground black pepper

Sautéed Wild Mushrooms (page 207)

3 tablespoons canola oil

**Four 6-ounce striped bass fillets,
    about 1¾ inches thick, skin on**

1 cup Wondra (see Note, page 140)

Preheat the oven to 400°F.

Spread the sweet potatoes on a baking sheet or in a Pyrex baking dish. Drizzle the ¼ cup olive oil over them, and season with 1/2 teaspoon each salt and pepper. Roast the potatoes until they're tender, about 25 minutes. Add them to the pan of Sautéed Wild Mushrooms, stir to combine, and keep warm over a low flame. (Leave the oven on.)

Heat the canola oil in a large, preferably nonstick, ovenproof sauté pan over a medium-high flame until hot but not smoking. Dry the fillets with paper towels and then season them with salt and pepper. Lightly dredge the skin side of the fillets in the flour and then add them, skin side down, to the sauté pan. Sear the fish for about 4 minutes, turn, and continue to cook for about 3 minutes. Transfer the pan to the oven and cook the fillets until they begin to flake when pressed with your finger, about 4 minutes more.

Serve the striped bass on four large plates with the sweet potatoes and Sautéed Wild Mushrooms alongside. Drizzle the plates with a little high-quality extra-virgin olive oil and a sprinkling of salt and freshly ground pepper.

John Dory with Leeks, Capers, and Saffron

The John Dory is often called St. Peter's fish because the matching black spots along its sides represent St. Peter's thumbprint. At Esca I make this dish with halibut (a similarly meaty, white-fleshed, mild fish), but it tastes just as good with John Dory, and it's a helluva lot cheaper. The leeks, capers, and saffron all melt together like a compote. The leeks are earthy, the capers are salty, and the saffron adds a final floral touch. **Serves 4**

2 large leeks	¼ cup capers (preferably salt-packed), rinsed
4 tablespoons (½ stick) unsalted butter	¼ cup chopped flat-leaf parsley
1 tablespoon extra-virgin olive oil	Four 6-ounce John Dory fillets
1 clove garlic, crushed	Sea salt
1 bay leaf	Freshly ground black pepper
¼ teaspoon saffron threads	3 tablespoons canola oil

Trace the diameter of a large sauté pan on a piece of parchment paper and cut it out. Split the leeks lengthwise, cut off any damaged green on top, and then slice the split leeks into ½-inch pieces. Place them in a bowl and rinse thoroughly with three changes of water. Drain; set aside.

In a large, straight-sided sauté pan, heat 3 tablespoons of the butter and the olive oil over a medium flame. Add the garlic and bay leaf, and cook for about 1 minute. When the garlic has softened, add the saffron and stir well. Add the capers. Sauté until the capers begin to bloom, then add ¼ cup water (the saffron will exude its color).

Add the reserved leeks and cover with the cut-out parchment paper. Gently simmer for about 20 minutes. The leeks should be tender and bright, moist but not wet; if there's too much liquid in the pan, remove the parchment and raise the flame slightly to reduce it. Add the parsley and stir to combine. Set the pan aside.

Season the fillets on both sides with salt and pepper.

Heat the canola oil in a large, preferably nonstick, pan until hot but not smoking. Add the remaining 1 tablespoon butter. When the foam subsides, add the fillets, with the smoother and better looking side down. Sear the fillets for about 4 minutes, until they are evenly brown, and then flip. Cook them for just 1 more minute, until they begin to flake when you press them with your finger. Transfer them to serving plates with the better-looking side up, spoon the reserved leeks over each, and season with a sprinkling of salt and freshly ground pepper.

Poached Sturgeon
with Cucumbers, Dill, and Mascarpone

Fresh sturgeon approximates the taste of meat even more than tuna steaks do. I've never had the fortune to catch one myself—not only are sturgeon a protected species but they weigh thousands of pounds and they don't like to be caught! Here, poaching the sturgeon gets it meltingly tender, like a slow-roasted pork shoulder. Salting the cucumbers for an hour gets a lot of the water out and firms them up, giving this dish some much needed crunch. The mascarpone cheese adds a luxurious creamy taste and sheen, but make sure you melt it only until it's warm all the way through, or it will break up. **Serves 4**

2 cucumbers, peeled, halved lengthwise, and cut into thin half moons

¹/₂ teaspoon sea salt

10 cups olive oil (see Note, page 191), plus high-quality extra-virgin olive oil, for drizzling

2 sprigs rosemary

1 dried árbol chile

1 clove garlic, crushed

Four 6-ounce sturgeon fillets

1 cup mascarpone

¹/₄ cup chopped dill

1 tablespoon pink peppercorns

Place the cucumber slices in a colander and sprinkle with the salt. Let sit for 1 hour.

In a Dutch oven or stockpot, combine the olive oil, rosemary, chile, and garlic. Bring to a gentle simmer over a medium-high flame.

Lower the fish into the oil and cook for 7 minutes. Use a slotted spoon to transfer the fillets to four serving plates.

While the fish is cooking, heat the mascarpone in a saucepan over a medium-low flame. Add the cucumbers, dill, and pink peppercorns, and fold together to combine. Keep the mixture warm over a low flame.

Serve the poached sturgeon with about ¹/₄ cup warm cucumber-mascarpone mixture spooned over the top of each fillet. I like to drizzle the plates with some high-quality extra-virgin olive oil before serving.

Pan-Roasted Cod
with Delicata Squashes and Braised Purple Cabbage

In the last couple of years, the cod stopped coming to my 'hood: they stopped making the right turn at Montauk. Maybe they're afraid of me because I catch so many. But it doesn't really matter—there are enough cod in the sea. The delicata squashes here are more savory than sweet; that quality makes them a fine foil for the sweet-fleshed cod. I love the way the butteriness of the fish plays off the astringent vinegary taste of the cabbage. **Serves 4**

2 delicata squashes (about 2 pounds total)

¼ cup extra-virgin olive oil

Sea salt

Freshly ground black pepper

4 sage leaves

Braised Purple Cabbage (page 143)

Four 6-ounce cod fillets,
    about 1¾ inches thick, skin on

1 cup Wondra (see Note, page 140)

3 tablespoons canola oil

Preheat the oven to 400°F.

To peel the squashes using a vegetable peeler: cut in half lengthwise, and spoon out and discard the seeds. Cut each half into wedges and then in half crosswise. Place the chunks on a baking sheet. Toss with the olive oil, 1 teaspoon each of salt and pepper, and the sage leaves. Bake until the squashes are very tender, about 30 minutes. Take out of the oven, leaving the heat on, and combine the tender squashes with the Braised Purple Cabbage.

Dry the fillets with paper towels. Season the flour with salt and pepper, and lightly dredge the skin side of the cod in the flour. Heat the canola oil in a large, preferably nonstick, sauté pan until the oil is almost smoking. Add the fish, skin side down, and sear for 4 minutes, until evenly browned. Turn and cook for 3 to 4 minutes more, then transfer to the still hot oven. Cook the fish until it begins to flake when you press your finger into it, 4 to 5 minutes more.

Spoon the squash-cabbage mixture into the center of four plates and top each with a cod fillet. Season each plate with a sprinkling of salt and freshly ground pepper, and serve immediately.

Cod with Early Fall Vegetables

In the fall, cod is at its firm-fleshed best, and when you combine the fish with some early fall vegetables the results are quite spectacular. This is an easy, versatile dish that's nevertheless worthy of being served to your family or company. **Serves 4**

2 small turnips, peeled

1 medium carrot, peeled

1 medium parsnip, peeled

1 small zucchini

1/4 cup extra-virgin olive oil

Sea salt

Freshly ground black pepper

Four 6-ounce cod fillets,
 about 1 3/4 inches thick, skin on

1 cup Wondra (see Note, page 140)

3 tablespoons canola oil

Preheat the oven to 350°F.

Cut all the vegetables into 3/4-inch chunks. Place them on a baking sheet, pour the olive oil over, and season with 1 teaspoon each salt and pepper. Toss the vegetables to combine, then spread them into a single layer. Roast in the oven until the vegetables are very tender when pierced with the tip of a knife, about 45 minutes. Transfer to a serving platter and keep warm.

Raise the oven temperature to 400°F.

Dry the cod fillets with paper towels. Season the flour with salt and pepper, then lightly dredge the skin side of the cod fillets in it. Heat the canola oil in a large, preferably nonstick, ovenproof sauté pan until the oil is almost smoking. Add the fillets, skin side down, and sear for 4 minutes, until evenly browned. Turn and cook for 3 to 4 minutes more, then transfer to the hot oven. Continue cooking until the fish begins to flake when you press your finger into it, 4 to 5 minutes.

Serve the cod over the roasted vegetables family-style. Be sure to put a bottle of high-quality extra-virgin olive oil and a dish of sea salt on the table so diners can season their plates.

"Okay, now here's a **SALMON.** Put your hand in the cavity— **YEAH,** right in the belly. Feel the oil? Well, that's what we're after."

King Salmon
with Sautéed Spinach and Cauliflower Puree

Last year I went fishing for king salmon off south Vancouver Island in British Columbia. Not only was the fishing amazing, but out on the water we spotted killer whales, as well as bears onshore and eagles soaring overhead. I like the way the earthiness of the cauliflower plays off the clean flavor of the salmon in this dish, and the spinach brings this whole thing together. Make sure you cook all the water out of the spinach, or you end up with a nasty-looking green puddle on the plate. **Serves 4**

2 cups whole milk

1 head cauliflower, split, core removed, florets separated

Sea salt

Freshly ground black pepper

Four 6-ounce king salmon fillets, skin on

3 tablespoons canola oil

1 tablespoon unsalted butter

Sautéed Spinach (recipe follows)

High-quality extra-virgin olive oil, for drizzling

Preheat the oven to 400°F.

Combine the milk with 1 cup water in a large, straight-sided sauté pan. Bring the liquid to a simmer over a medium flame. Add the cauliflower florets and season with 1/2 teaspoon salt and a few turns of a pepper mill. Simmer the cauliflower, stirring occasionally, until it is very tender, about 15 minutes.

While the cauliflower is simmering, dry the salmon fillets with paper towels and season them with salt and pepper. Heat the canola oil in a large, preferably nonstick, ovenproof sauté pan over a medium flame. Add the butter. When the foam subsides, add the salmon, skin side down. Sear the salmon for about 3 minutes, turn, and sear the other side for about 3 minutes more. Transfer the pan to the oven. Finish cooking the fish about 4 minutes more in the oven, until it begins to flake when you press it with your finger.

Transfer the cauliflower and its cooking liquid to a blender. Puree until smooth. Pour into four small bowls, and season with salt and pepper.

Serve the salmon on large individual plates, with the Sautéed Spinach alongside, and the small bowls of cauliflower puree sitting on the plates. Drizzle with high-quality extra-virgin olive oil and season with a sprinkling of salt and pepper. Serve immediately.

Sautéed Spinach

You can serve this Sautéed Spinach with just about any dish in the book. Let's face it—you can't go wrong with Sautéed Spinach. Popeye never did. **Serves 4**

½ **cup extra-virgin olive oil**

5 **cloves garlic, thinly sliced**

4 **pounds spinach, washed, spun-dry, and stemmed**

Juice of 1 lemon

½ **teaspoon sea salt**

Freshly ground black pepper

Heat half the olive oil in a large, straight-sided sauté pan over a medium-high flame. Add the garlic and cook until it softens and begins to take on color, about 4 minutes. Add the spinach and use tongs to continually toss it in the olive oil so that the leaves begin to wilt. Remove from the heat and add the lemon juice, the salt, and a few turns of a pepper mill. Continue to toss. Drizzle the spinach with the remaining olive oil before serving alongside the salmon.

Pacific wild salmon run from May through September. These are the most common varieties:

- **Copper River salmon** is the first wild salmon of the season that makes it to New York. It's good salmon—don't get me wrong—but it's just way overpriced.

- **Sockeye salmon** are small, lean, very bright red-fleshed fish, with a clean, almost vegetal taste. They're not very fatty, and it's the only salmon species that hasn't been farmed. The Japanese love them so much they often drive the price of sockeye through the roof.

- **King salmon** (also known as Chinook) is the most widely available high-quality wild salmon. Its flesh color ranges from off-white to bright red. King salmon vary widely in size, from 10 to 50-plus pounds.

- **Albino or white salmon** are one of my favorite wild salmon, but even I have a hard time getting a hold of it. It tastes a little like bass. White salmon's got great fat content. Its color ranges from light pink to bone china white.

- **Farmed Atlantic salmon** represents over 90 percent of the salmon sold in the United States. All Atlantic salmon is farmed. Atlantic farmed salmon has a fairly high fat content and delicate pink meat, and tastes only vaguely of the sea. In fact, I think it tastes like soybeans. Atlantic salmon is farmed in Canada, Chile, and Maine.

- Companies are starting to offer **farmed Pacific salmon** as well. I've never bought it, as much on principle as anything else. Apparently the farmed Pacific salmon escape their pens and screw up the genetics of the wild salmon.

Important Note: It's almost impossible to tell the difference between farmed and wild salmon just by looking. Both varieties come in various shades of red and pink. Wild salmon become pink by eating sea creatures, which contain astaxanthin. Farmed salmon are naturally grayish but turn pink when they are fed various sources of astaxanthin. Marian Burros of *The New York Times* wrote a fascinating story a couple of years ago about the number of high-end stores and restaurants in New York City that unwittingly buy farm-raised salmon that are labeled wild. I'm sure I've been fooled on occasion.

Pan-Roasted Striped Bass with Lentils

I always think of New Year's Day when I think of this dish, because eating lentils on January 1st is supposed to bring you wealth and prosperity—each lentil you eat represents some increment of the money you are going to make for the year. Donna and I eat a lot of lentils every New Year's Day. I cook my lentils like risotto: I don't soak them first because I believe that process leaches out much of the lentil's flavor; instead, I keep on adding liquid to the pan. You need a hearty fish for this dish, and tuna or salmon or even cod work just as well as the striped bass. **Serves 4**

2 tablespoons extra-virgin olive oil,
    plus high-quality extra-virgin
    olive oil, for drizzling

2 ounces pancetta, cut into a small dice

1 medium carrot, cut into a small dice

1 stalk celery, cut into a small dice

8 ounces dried lentils

1 bay leaf

Sea salt

Freshly ground black pepper

3 tablespoons canola oil

Four 6-ounce striped bass fillets,
    1¾ inches thick, skin on (see headnote)

1 cup Wondra (see Note, page 140)

In a medium saucepan, heat the 2 tablespoons olive oil over a medium flame. Add the pancetta and cook, stirring frequently, until it is lightly browned and much of the fat has been rendered, 5 to 7 minutes. Add the carrot and celery and continue to cook until they have softened, about 15 minutes. Add the lentils and toss to coat with the olive oil and vegetables. Cook for 2 to 3 minutes, then add the bay leaf and 2 cups water. Bring the liquid to a simmer (raise the flame slightly) and continue to cook, stirring frequently, until the lentils have absorbed the liquid, about 15 minutes. Add another 2 cups water and continue cooking and stirring until the lentils are very tender, about 20 minutes more. The lentils should be fairly wet. Add salt and pepper to taste.

Preheat the oven to 400°F.

Heat the canola oil in a large, preferably nonstick, ovenproof sauté pan over a medium-high flame until hot but not smoking. Dry the fillets with paper towels and then season them with 1 teaspoon salt and $1/2$ teaspoon pepper. Lightly dredge the skin side of the fillets in the flour and then add them, skin side down, to the sauté pan. Sear the fish for about 4 minutes. Turn and continue to cook for about 3 minutes more. Transfer the pan to the oven and cook the fillets until they begin to flake when pressed with your finger, about 4 minutes more.

Spoon the lentils into four shallow bowls and place a fillet in the center of each. Drizzle each bowl with high-quality extra-virgin olive oil and a sprinkling of salt and freshly ground pepper.

Red Mullets
with Figs and Pistachios

A lot of fish lovers don't like red mullets because they're small, bony fish with a distinctive minerally, sealike flavor. I think they're one of the great Mediterranean fish, with a delicious, distinctive sweet flavor. Use fresh figs here because the dried variety will impart an unwanted candylike sweetness to the dish. As for the pistachios, which lend a Mediterranean flair as well as some crunch, make sure you buy the unsalted kind. **Serves 4**

¼ cup roasted unsalted pistachio nuts, shelled

3 tablespoons extra-virgin olive oil, plus high-quality extra-virgin olive oil, for drizzling

8 red mullets, cleaned

1 lemon, sliced

4 bay leaves

8 sprigs thyme

1 cup Wondra (see Note, page 140)

8 fresh Black Mission figs, halved

Sea salt

Freshly ground black pepper

Preheat the oven to 350°F. Spread the pistachios on a baking sheet and toast them for 3 to 5 minutes, until fragrant and lightly brown. Set aside.

Raise the oven temperature to 400°F.

Heat 3 tablespoons of the olive oil in a large straight-sided ovenproof sauté pan over a medium-high flame until hot but not smoking.

Stuff the cavity of each mullet with a slice of lemon, half a bay leaf, and a sprig of thyme. Dredge each fish in the flour, and transfer to the hot sauté pan. Cook until golden, about 4 minutes. Flip the fish and add the figs and reserved toasted nuts to the pan. Transfer the pan to the oven and cook for about 4 minutes more, until the mullets begin to flake when you press them with your finger.

Serve the mullets, two per person, with the split figs and a sprinkling of pistachios. Season with salt and pepper, and finish with a generous drizzling of high-quality olive oil.

Monkfish
with Cauliflower Stewed with Saffron and Gaeta Olives

Monkfish has a lobsterlike texture with a mild flavor that's perfect for these more assertive ingredients, plus it's usually a bargain. It has the advantages of being resilient, forgiving, and virtually impossible to overcook. Here it's the centerpiece of a great one-pot dish that works beautifully for a dinner party. You can prepare it ahead of time, and the yellow saffron and the Gaeta olives make for a very colorful dish. **Serves 4**

Extra-virgin olive oil

½ yellow onion, diced

2 cloves garlic, thinly sliced

1 dried mild red chile
(such as Italian finger hots)

½ cup Gaeta olives, pitted

¼ teaspoon saffron threads

1 head cauliflower, broken into florets

Four 6-ounce monkfish tails

1 cup Wondra (see Note, page 140)

Sea salt

Freshly ground black pepper

3 tablespoons canola oil

Trace the diameter of a sauté pan onto parchment paper and cut it out.

Heat some olive oil in the sauté pan over a medium flame. Add the onion, garlic, and chile and cook until the onion is translucent, about 3 minutes. Add the olives and stir to combine, then add 1 cup water and the saffron threads. Raise the flame to medium high, bring to a simmer, and add the cauliflower. Stir well so that the cauliflower turns the color of the saffron. Cover with the parchment-paper round and simmer until the cauliflower is very tender, about 20 minutes.

Preheat the oven to 400°F.

Dry the monkfish with paper towels. Season the flour with salt and pepper, and lightly dredge the monkfish in it.

Heat the canola oil in a large, preferably nonstick, ovenproof skillet over a medium-high flame. Add the monkfish and sear 3 minutes per side, then transfer to the oven for 4 minutes more. Transfer the cooked monkfish to four serving plates. Serve immediately with the stewed cauliflower alongside.

Yellowtail with Spaghetti Squash, Oven-Dried Tomatoes, and Vin Cotto

This is an elegant version of a similar dish I make with cod—I love how these flavors go together. The yellowtail is an absolutely lovely and special fish, with a great satiny texture. It's a warm-weather fish caught in the South and in California that the Japanese love to use for sushi. Vin cotto is cooked grape must, which has the consistency of honey. **Serves 4**

1 large spaghetti squash (about 4 pounds)	**6 Oven-Dried Tomatoes (page 205)**
Extra-virgin olive oil	**¼ cup canola oil**
Sea salt	**Four 6-ounce yellowtail fillets**
Freshly ground black pepper	**4 tablespoons vin cotto**

Preheat the oven to 400°F.

Cut the squash lengthwise, through the stem, and scoop out and discard the seeds. Drizzle the flesh side with olive oil and season with salt and pepper. Line a baking sheet with parchment paper or aluminum foil and place the squash, cut side down, on the paper. Bake until completely soft when pierced with a fork, 45 to 50 minutes. Cool the squash for about 15 minutes, then scoop out the flesh and mix gently with the Oven-Dried Tomatoes.

Heat the canola oil in a large, preferably nonstick, sauté pan until hot. Add the fillets. Cook the fish for 5 to 6 minutes total. I don't flip these. The edges will start to appear opaque as the fillets cook from the bottom up.

Serve on four individual plates with the squash-tomato mixture alongside. Drizzle a little vin cotto in a circle around both.

Slow-Roasted Hake with Purple Cauliflower Sicilian-Style

If I didn't think I'd get in trouble with the Pope, I would call raisins, pine nuts, and capers the holy trinity of Sicilian cooking. The Sicilians put them on just about anything, from vegetables to fish and chicken, and so will you once you try it. Here I pair the versatile trio with cauliflower and hake, which is a cheaper, codlike fish. **Serves 4**

2 tablespoons pine nuts

1 head purple cauliflower

5 tablespoons extra-virgin olive oil, plus high-quality extra-virgin olive oil, for drizzling

1 small yellow onion, finely diced (about ½ cup)

1 tablespoon capers, drained

2 tablespoons white raisins

¼ cup dry white wine

Sea salt

Freshly ground black pepper

Leaves of 4 sprigs flat-leaf parsley

Four 6-ounce hake fillets

1 cup Wondra (see Note, page 140)

3 tablespoons canola oil

Preheat the oven to 300°F. Place the nuts in a shallow baking dish and toast them in the oven for 2 minutes (they burn quickly). Set aside, leaving the oven on.

Cut the head of cauliflower in half, core, and remove the florets.

Heat 3 tablespoons of the olive oil in a straight-sided sauté pan over a medium flame until hot but not smoking. Add the diced onion and cook until softened, about 4 minutes, stirring occasionally. Add the capers, raisins, and wine. Stir to coat the ingredients with the oil and cook for about 2 minutes so the raisins can absorb the wine.

Add the cauliflower florets along with ½ cup water. Season with ½ teaspoon salt and some freshly ground pepper. Adjust the heat so the liquid in the pan is gently bubbling, and cover with a lid, leaving a slight opening. Cook until the cauliflower is tender, 20 to 25 minutes. Stir frequently and monitor the liquid in the pan. If it bubbles away entirely, add 1 or 2 more tablespoons water. Taste to test for tenderness.

Raise the oven temperature to 400°F.

Add the pine nuts and the remaining 2 tablespoons olive oil to the cauliflower. Mix to incorporate, and heat for an additional 3 minutes. Transfer to a serving bowl and garnish with the parsley leaves.

Dry the hake fillets with paper towels. Season the flour with salt and pepper and lightly dredge the fillets.

Heat the canola oil in a large, preferably nonstick, ovenproof sauté pan until hot. Add the fillets, better-looking side down, to the pan. Sear the fish for 3 to 4 minutes per side, until nicely browned, and then transfer to the oven. Cook for 3 to 4 minutes more, until the fish begins to flake when you press it with your finger.

Drizzle the fillets with some high-quality extra-virgin olive oil and a sprinkling of salt. Serve the hake immediately with the stewed cauliflower alongside and enjoy.

Olive Oil-Poached Halibut with Roasted Beets and Blood Oranges

Poaching fish in olive oil gives it a luxe texture. Don't think the fish is going to be oily or greasy as a result because it's not. In fact, poaching—the gentlest form of cooking—gives the fish a terrific, clean flavor. Halibut is fairly bland, so it needs the flavor intensity that the beets and blood oranges supply. **Serves 4**

2 blood oranges

8 whole golden Roasted Beets (recipe follows)

10 cups olive oil (see Preparation Note), plus high-quality extra-virgin olive oil, for drizzling.

1 sprig rosemary

1 clove garlic, crushed

1 dried árbol chile

Sea salt

Four 6-ounce halibut fillets

Freshly ground black pepper

Use a chef's knife to slice the tops and bottoms off the blood oranges so they sit flat on a cutting board. Cut the peel away from the flesh in wide strips from top to bottom. Hold the fruit over a bowl (to catch the juice) and cut each segment away from the membrane. Combine the blood orange segments and the roasted beets with the orange juice in the bowl.

In a Dutch oven or stockpot, combine the 10 cups olive oil, rosemary, garlic, chile, and salt. Heat the oil over a medium-high flame to a gentle simmer, then use a slotted spoon to remove the rosemary, garlic, and chile, and discard.

Lower the fish into the oil and cook for 5 to 6 minutes for medium-rare (the way I like it) or 7 minutes for medium.

While the fish is poaching, place four slices of blood orange on each of four serving plates. Sprinkle with a little salt and pepper.

Use a slotted spoon to transfer the cooked fillets to the serving plates, resting on the blood orange slices. Put four beet halves on each plate. Drizzle the fish and the beets with some high-quality extra-virgin olive oil and a fine sprinkling of salt and freshly ground pepper. Serve immediately.

PREPARATION NOTE

I know you're using a lot of olive oil to poach in, but because the temperature of the oil never gets very high, you can reuse the oil for frying.

Roasted Beets

The only way I like beets is roasted. Even beet haters go for these. **Serves 4**

6 medium beets
Extra-virgin olive oil
Sea salt
Freshly ground black pepper

Preheat the oven to 400°F.

Trim the top end of each beet, then roll it in a puddle of olive oil. Season each with salt. Wrap the beets individually in aluminum foil, place on a baking sheet, and bake until they are easily pierced with the tip of a knife, about 1 hour. Remove from the oven. When cool enough to handle, remove the skins. Slice and season to taste.

The beets can be roasted ahead of time and then refrigerated. Keep them wrapped in foil and bring to room temperature before using.

Hake
di Salerno

I visited Salerno, a seaside town near Naples famous for its limoncello, in order to take the ferry to Capri, with my wife and Molto (Mario Batali) a few years ago. I noticed that every restaurant used virtually the same preparation for everything, from chicken to shrimp to fish. For this recipe I use hake, because it's a versatile, reasonably priced fish, but feel free to make the dish with cod or scrod or even lemon or gray sole. Make the bread crumbs at home or buy the best-quality crumbs you can find. *Note:* Using a nonstick casserole is essential for this dish. I use a Le Creuset cast-iron pan with an enamel coating. **Serves 4**

1½ **pounds new potatoes (red or white)**

4 **cloves garlic, 2 whole and 2 thinly sliced**

½ **cup basil leaves**

¼ **cup flat-leaf parsley leaves**

½ **teaspoon sea salt**

½ **teaspoon freshly ground black pepper**

½ **loaf stale Pulman bread, crust off**

Four 8-ounce local hake fillets

Extra-virgin olive oil, for drizzling

Juice of 3 lemons

4 **tablespoons (**½ **stick) unsalted butter, melted**

Place the potatoes in a large saucepan of salted water and bring to a boil. Cook the potatoes for about 10 minutes, until soft when pierced with a paring knife but still firm enough to keep their shape. Drain. When cool enough to handle, remove the skins and cut each in half.

Preheat the oven to 450°F.

In a mini food processor, combine the 2 whole cloves garlic and half the basil with the parsley, salt, and pepper. Add the bread in small pieces and pulse until the mixture is bright green. Set aside.

Place the potatoes and the sliced garlic in an earthenware baking dish. Place three basil leaves in the center of each fillet and roll up the fillet. Place the fillets on top of the potatoes, seam side down so they stay rolled. Drizzle the olive oil and lemon juice over the fish, and top with the reserved seasoned bread crumbs and the melted butter.

Cook in the oven for 10 to 15 minutes, until the fish begins to flake when you press it with your finger. Serve immediately.

Crispy

Steamers with Caper-Tarragon Aioli

This is an Ed Levine–inspired dish. Ed likes fried clams more than life itself, and frankly I do, too. Who doesn't? There's this great fried clam place near my house, Bigelow's, that Ed and I go to all the time, and this dish is my attempt to replicate their delicious fried clams (see page 198). Steamers fry up beautifully, but you can use littlenecks or cherrystones just as easily. I pot-fry the clams, using a candy thermometer to monitor the temperature of the oil. The Caper-Tarragon Aioli is just a really tasty elegant tartar sauce. Unlike traditional aioli, I don't use any garlic. **Serves 4**

FOR THE CAPER-TARRAGON AIOLI

3 large egg yolks

1 tablespoon fresh lemon juice

1/4 teaspoon cayenne pepper

1 teaspoon tarragon, leaves only

1 teaspoon flat-leaf parsley, leaves only

3/4 cup canola oil

1/2 cup extra-virgin olive oil

1 hard-boiled egg, yolk and white separated and chopped

2 teaspoons capers (preferably salt-packed)

FOR THE STEAMERS

Sea salt

24 medium steamers

6 cups extra-virgin olive oil

2 cups canola oil

1 1/2 cups Wondra (see Note, page 140)

1 cup cornstarch

Pinch of sugar

Pinch of cayenne pepper

Freshly ground black pepper

MAKE THE AIOLI

Put the egg yolks, lemon juice, cayenne, tarragon, and parsley in a blender or food processor. With the machine running, add the 3/4 cup canola oil and the 1/2 cup olive oil in a slow, steady stream (this should take about 2 minutes). Process until a thick, creamy emulsion forms. Transfer to a small mixing bowl, then add the hard-boiled egg and capers, folding them in gently with a rubber spatula. This aioli can be covered and refrigerated for up to 3 days.

MAKE THE STEAMERS AND SAUCE

Prepare a large bowl of ice water with about 1/4 cup salt in it. Shuck the clams and reserve the juice in a jar or container. Split the necks, then peel and discard the membranes (you can ask your fishmonger to do this for you). Place the steamers in the ice water for 10 minutes to draw the sand from them.

Combine the 6 cups olive oil and 2 cups canola oil in a Dutch oven or stockpot. There should be 8 inches of oil. If there isn't, add more to bring it to that depth. Set the pot over a medium flame. Using a candy thermometer, bring the oil to 275°F and maintain that temperature.

In a wide mixing bowl, while the oil is heating, combine the flour, cornstarch, sugar, cayenne, and 2 teaspoons each salt and pepper.

Dredge the steamers in the flour mixture, shaking off the excess before gently lowering the pieces into the hot oil (use tongs or a slotted spoon). The pieces should bubble and sizzle but not spatter; lower or raise the heat accordingly. Cook four to six pieces at a time until they are golden brown and crisp, about 5 minutes. Use a slotted spoon to transfer the steamers to a paper-towel-lined tray. Season with salt and pepper while the pieces are still hot out of the oil.

Bigelow's:
My Fried Clam Shack

If you live as close to the water as I do, there's always a fried clam joint to call your own. In my case it's Bigelow's, and I've been eating their fantastic fried clams and French fries since my dad took me there 30 years ago. My fried clam recipe is a little more fancy-pants than Bigelow's, but I'm not going to say it's better, because at Bigelow's you get a side order of salt air gratis, and we don't have salt air on the menu at Esca.

Bigelow's is a simple, no-frills kind of place, as a fried clam joint should be. It's one horseshoe counter with an island of fryers and a grill. Perfect fried clams have been made in this location for more than 60 years. According to its take-out menu, "It was the year 1939, and a young man by the name of Russ Bigelow came to Rockville Centre, Long Island, to open a seafood restaurant at 79 North Long Beach Road (516-678-3878). While working in the hotels of New England, Russ learned the true art of frying seafood. He brought this with him and in the process introduced the Ipswich clam, also known as the soft-shell clam, to Long Island."

Russ Bigelow retired in 1964 and sold the store to one of his employees, Tom Brown. Brown retired in 1991 and sold Bigelow's to the current owners, the Andreolas family, Spiro and his three sons. They've added some grilled seafood and chicken items to the menu, but the Andreolases have wisely maintained the fried clam traditions of Russ Bigelow.

Each order of fried clams is dredged in an egg wash, then dipped in flour and fried to order. What comes out of those fryers are perfect, nutty fried clams,

with full if supermodel-sized bellies and just a hint of sweetness. They are crisp and greaseless, and just need a shake of salt to achieve fried clam high art. The clams come with French fries that are also part of the Bigelow suburban legend.

After the fries come out of the fryer, one of the cooks places the entire order in a cloth napkin with some salt, twists the cloth napkin closed so nothing can escape, and shakes and twirls the napkin to drain the fries and distribute the salt.

My dad first took me to Bigelow's when I was about ten. I've taken my little Ruby to Bigelow's hoping she'll take to the perfect fried clams and the horseshoe counter. So far Bigelow's appeal has eluded Ruby, but as I write this she's only two. She's got time to discover Bigelow's magic, and I'm sure she will.

Fritto Misto Amalfitano

Every port in Italy has a fried-fish combination plate, but not too many have good ones. On the Amalfi Coast, however, they know how to do fried seafood right. The key is to make sure the oil is at the right temperature. I fry fish at 275°F., which is at least 100 degrees lower than what most people do. I also use a combination of half olive oil and half vegetable or peanut oil: the lower temperature and the oil combination keeps the fish crispy on the outside and moist on the inside. Use whatever fish looks best at your local market. The fried lemon slices, which I first saw on the Amalfi Coast, are a great touch. **Serves 4**

6 cups extra-virgin olive oil

2 cups canola oil

1½ cups Wondra (see Note, page 140)

1 cup cornstarch

Pinch of sugar

Pinch of cayenne pepper

Sea salt

Freshly ground black pepper

1 pound squid, cut into 1½-inch pieces

4 ounces shucked oysters

4 ounces bay scallops

½ pound scrod, cut into 1¼-inch strips

2 lemons, 1 thinly sliced and 1 cut into wedges

Combine the olive and canola oils in a Dutch oven or stockpot. There should be 8 inches of oil. If there isn't, add more to bring it to that depth. Set the pot over a medium flame. Using a thermometer, bring the oil to 275°F and maintain that temperature.

In a wide mixing bowl, while the oil is heating, combine the flour, cornstarch, sugar, cayenne, and 2 teaspoons each of salt and pepper. Dredge the fish and the lemon slices, a few pieces at a time, in the flour mixture, shaking off the excess before gently lowering the pieces into the hot oil (use tongs or a slotted spoon). The pieces should bubble and sizzle but not spatter; lower or raise the flame accordingly. Cook four to six pieces at a time until they are golden brown and crisp, about 5 minutes. (While cooking the fish, keep an eye on the oil temperature. It will drop after the raw ingredients are added and climb while they are cooking. Do not let it climb above 280°F.) Use a slotted spoon to transfer to a paper-towel-lined tray. Season with salt and pepper while the pieces are still hot out of the oil.

After the cooked fish and lemon slices have drained, serve, family-style, garnished with the lemon wedges.

Ruby Red Shrimp
with Artichokes, Capers, and Mint

A Venetian coming home from work often stops in at a *cicchetti* for a glass of wine and just points at the food he wants. These bars serve prepared items like this kind of dish at room temperature. But I think crispy foods are best served hot. The ruby red shrimp, from Maine, are in season in the winter, but feel free to use Gulf shrimp, which are available year-round. I use a little flour mixed with cornstarch to give it an airier crispiness. **Serves 4**

6 cups extra-virgin olive oil

2 cups canola oil

1½ cups Wondra (see Note, page 140)

1 cup cornstarch

Pinch of sugar

Pinch of cayenne

Sea salt

Freshly ground black pepper

4 sprigs rosemary

2 sprigs mint

4 baby artichokes, green outer leaves removed, thinly sliced across the heart

1 pound ruby red shrimp, heads and shells on, antennae trimmed

3 tablespoons capers

Combine the olive and canola oils in a Dutch oven or stockpot. There should be 8 inches of oil. If there isn't, add more to bring it to that depth. Set the pot over a medium flame. Using a thermometer, bring the oil to 275°F and maintain that temperature.

In a wide mixing bowl, while the oil is heating, combine the flour, cornstarch, sugar, cayenne, and 2 teaspoons each of salt and pepper.

Put the rosemary and mint sprigs into the oil and deep-fry until the needles are crispy, about 3 minutes. Transfer them to a paper-towel-lined serving platter.

Add the artichokes and fry until golden, about 5 minutes. Transfer them to the serving platter and season with salt and pepper while still hot.

Dredge the shrimp in the flour mixture, shaking off the excess before gently lowering the pieces into the hot oil (use tongs or a slotted spoon). The pieces should bubble and sizzle but not spatter; lower or raise the heat accordingly. Cook four to six pieces at a time until golden brown and crisp, about 5 minutes. Use a slotted spoon to transfer to the paper-towel-lined platter with the artichokes. Season with salt and pepper while the pieces are still hot out of the oil. Add the capers to the hot oil and fry them for about 1 minute. Use a slotted spoon to remove them. Serve everything immediately.

Flounder with Beets and Sugar Snap Peas

Fried flounder was the first fish our parents tried to get most of us to eat—which makes sense given its mild taste and firm texture. This flounder preparation is for adults and kids alike. Peas and mint are a classic French springtime combination, and they lend any dish a zippy, clean, fresh taste. The beets, which can and should be made the day before, provide an earthy, just sweet enough touch. **Serves 4**

1 pound beets, scrubbed and dried

½ cup extra-virgin olive oil, plus more for drizzling

Sea salt

Freshly ground black pepper

¼ cup mint leaves

1 cup Italian-Style Bread Crumbs (page 233) or high-quality store-bought bread crumbs

1 cup Wondra (see Note, page 140)

3 large eggs

Four 5-ounce flounder fillets

1 pound sugar snap peas

¼ cup canola oil

3 tablespoons unsalted butter

Preheat the oven to 350°F.

Place each beet on a square of aluminum foil. Drizzle with olive oil, roll the beet to lightly coat, and season with a sprinkling of salt and pepper. Wrap loosely in the foil. Place the packets on a baking sheet and then in the oven. Roast until the beets are easily pierced with the point of a knife, about 1 hour. Remove from the oven and let cool. When cool enough to handle, peel and cut into a ½-inch dice. Set aside.

Finely chop half the mint leaves. In a shallow bowl, combine them with the bread crumbs. In another shallow bowl, season the Wondra with 1 teaspoon each salt and pepper. In a third bowl, lightly beat the eggs. Dredge each flounder fillet in the seasoned flour, then dip in the beaten egg, and then in the bread crumbs. Set aside on a baking sheet.

In a large sauté pan, heat the ½ cup olive oil. Add the sugar snap peas and sauté until tender, about 5 minutes. Add the diced beets and the reserved unchopped mint and continue cooking for 1 minute.

In another large, preferably nonstick, sauté pan, heat the canola oil until hot but not smoking. Add the butter. When the foam subsides, add the fillets; you should hear them sizzle. Cook until golden brown, about 3 to 4 minutes per side. Transfer the cooked fillets to a paper-towel-lined platter and season immediately with salt and pepper. Serve with the sugar snap peas and beets alongside.

Flounder with Baby Eggplant, Oven-Dried Tomatoes, and Grilled Sweet Onions

The key to this summery dish is to find small eggplant with tender skins and without seeds. The tomatoes add a little acidity that balances the richness of the rest of the dish, and the grilled sweet onions add great texture and sweetness. Leave the onions crunchy, and don't cook them too long. I add a little butter to the pan after I've put the fish in just to give the flounder a luxurious taste. **Serves 4**

8 baby Italian eggplant, halved lengthwise

Sea salt

¼ cup extra-virgin olive oil, plus additional for drizzling

4 sprigs rosemary

2 Maui onions, cut into ½-inch slices

1 cup Wondra (see Note, page 140)

Freshly ground black pepper

3 large eggs

Four 5-ounce flounder fillets

¼ cup canola oil

3 tablespoons unsalted butter

Oven-Dried Tomatoes (recipe follows)

Sprinkle the cut side of the eggplant with salt. Layer them face down in a colander for 30 minutes to drain some of their water.

Preheat the oven to 350°F.

Place the eggplant, cut side up, on a baking sheet and drizzle liberally with olive oil. Break the sprigs of rosemary into pieces and place them on top of the eggplant. Transfer to the oven and bake until very tender, 30 to 35 minutes.

While the eggplant are cooking, lightly coat the onion slices with olive oil and sprinkle with salt and pepper. Grill over a charcoal fire or heat in a grill pan over a medium-high flame for 3 minutes per side.

Set two wide shallow bowls near the stove. In one, season the flour with 1 teaspoon each salt and pepper. In the other, lightly beat the eggs. Dredge each flounder in the seasoned flour, then dip in the beaten egg. Set each aside on a baking sheet.

In a large, preferably nonstick, sauté pan, heat the canola oil over a medium-high flame until hot but not smoking. Add the butter. When the foam subsides, add the fillets. As they sizzle, carefully use your fingertips to press them down, giving them full contact with the pan. After 2 minutes, give them a quarter turn to the right. Cook until golden brown, 3 to 4 minutes per side. Transfer the cooked fillets to a paper-towel-lined plate and season immediately with salt and pepper. Serve with the Oven-Dried Tomatoes, two eggplant halves, and a few slices of grilled onion.

Oven-Dried Tomatoes

Where I live and cook, in the Northeast, the vine-ripened tomato season is really short. So the way I compensate is by making these Oven-Dried Tomatoes, which sweeten just about any plum or Roma tomato you can find year-round. **Serves 4**

1 pound plum or Roma tomatoes
¼ cup extra-virgin olive oil
Leaves of 2 sprigs thyme

Sea salt
Freshly ground black pepper

Preheat the oven to 300°F.

Bring a large pot of water to a boil and prepare a bowl of ice water near the stove. Use a paring knife to score an X on the bottom of each tomato, and use the tip of the knife to carve out the stem end.

Put the tomatoes in the boiling water for 3 minutes, then use a slotted spoon to transfer them to the ice bath. Starting at the X, peel the skins away from the flesh.

Cut each tomato in half lengthwise, and remove and discard the seeds. Place the flesh in a mixing bowl. Add the olive oil and thyme, and season with salt and pepper. Toss to thoroughly coat the tomatoes. Place them, cut side down, on a foil-lined baking sheet. Pour any excess dressing over them and then bake for 1½ hours. When finished, the tomatoes should have shrunk and become a brighter shade of red.

The tomatoes can be used immediately or stored in the refrigerator in an airtight container for 3 days. Let come to room temperature before using.

Skate with Sautéed Wild Mushrooms and Brussels Sprouts

Skate is actually a nasty-looking sea ray. We eat the wings only. The rest of the skate is inedible and tough to look at. To my way of thinking, skate has to be served crispy. I fry it in a shallow pan with a combination of vegetable oil and butter, for the flavor the butter imparts and the clean taste things get when fried in vegetable oil. I use Wondra for this dish because it gets a really crisp edge without tasting floury. The pancetta, which I roast with the Brussels sprouts, gives the dish a little smoky, porky, tinge. **Serves 4**

Sea salt

¾ pound Brussels sprouts,
    outer leaves discarded, quartered

4 ounces slab pancetta, diced

Freshly ground black pepper

Sautéed Wild Mushrooms (recipe follows)

1½ cups Wondra (see Note, page 140)

1 cup cornstarch

1 cup whole milk

Four 6-ounce skate wings

¼ cup canola oil

5 tablespoons unsalted butter

Aceto balsamico (aged balsamic vinegar),
    for drizzling

Bring a large pot of salted water to a boil. Plunge the Brussels sprouts into the water and cook until tender, about 5 minutes. Drain and rinse in cold water. Set aside.

In a sauté pan, brown the pancetta over a medium flame until almost crisp, about 5 minutes. Add the Brussels sprouts and mix to combine and coat the Brussels sprouts with the fat. Season with about ½ teaspoon each salt and pepper. Add the Sautéed Wild Mushrooms, stir to combine, and keep warm over a low flame.

Set two wide shallow bowls near the stove. In one, combine the flour and cornstarch and season with 1 teaspoon each salt and pepper. Pour the milk into the other bowl. Dip each skate wing into the milk, then lightly dredge in the flour mixture. Repeat with another dip in the milk and a final dredging in the flour.

Heat the canola oil in a large sauté pan over a high flame until hot but not smoking. Add the butter. When the foam subsides, add the skate wings. As they sizzle, carefully use your fingertips or a wooden spoon to press them down, giving them full contact with the pan. After 2 minutes, give them a quarter turn to the right. Cook until golden brown, about 3 minutes per side (turn the wings carefully so they don't break apart). Transfer the cooked wings to a paper-towel-lined plate and season immediately with salt and pepper. Serve the skate wings with the warm Brussels sprouts and mushrooms spooned into the inner curve of the wing, and a little *aceto balsamico* drizzled over everything.

Sautéed Wild Mushrooms

I make Sautéed Wild Mushrooms instead of braised ones when I want to add a little caramelized crunch to the plate. Use oyster mushrooms, porcini, hen of the woods, black trumpet, or even button mushrooms for this recipe. **Serves 4**

¼ cup extra-virgin olive oil

1 pound assorted wild mushrooms

1 teaspoon salt

½ teaspoon freshly ground black pepper

Juice of 1 lemon
    (omit if using black trumpet mushrooms)

In a large sauté pan, heat the olive oil over a medium-high flame. When the pan is hot, place the mushrooms to cover the surface (the pan should still be roomy), and toss to coat in the oil; do this in batches if necessary. Season with the salt and pepper, and let the mushrooms sit, undisturbed, for about 2 minutes, before turning. When the mushrooms have softened and browned, add a squeeze of lemon juice, toss to coat, and remove from the heat. Repeat, if necessary, until all the mushrooms are cooked. Serve hot or at room temperature.

Cod with Lemon Jam

I love this lemon jam so much I use it to accompany just about anything fried, from cod to shrimp and scallops. Here I cook with lemon the way the Italians do. They would call the lemon jam *marmalata,* and you can, too. Just puree the whole fruit, zest and skin and all. If you find Meyer lemons, you don't have to use sugar. **Serves 4**

4 lemons, preferably Meyer, washed

1/2 cup extra-virgin olive oil

1/2 teaspoon red pepper flakes

1 teaspoon sugar, or more to taste

Four 6-ounce cod fillets

Sea salt

Freshly ground black pepper

1 1/2 cups Wondra (see Note, page 140)

1 cup cornstarch

1 cup whole milk

1/4 cup canola oil

3 tablespoons unsalted butter

Remove the stem ends of the lemons and cut them into 1-inch chunks, skins included. Combine the chopped lemons, olive oil, red pepper flakes and sugar in a blender. Pulse until it's the texture of a relish; add 1 or 2 tablespoons water if it's too thick.

Season the cod fillets with salt and pepper.

Set two wide shallow bowls near the stove. In one, combine the flour and cornstarch, and season with 1 teaspoon each salt and pepper; pour the milk into the other bowl. Dip each fillet into the milk, then lightly dredge in the flour mixture.

Heat the canola oil in a large sauté pan over a medium-high flame until hot but not smoking. Add the butter. When the foam subsides, add the cod fillets. Cook until golden brown, about 4 minutes per side. Transfer the cooked fillets to a paper-towel-lined plate and season immediately with salt and pepper.

Serve the fillets immediately, with the lemon jam spooned over the center.

Skate with Grapes and Cherry Tomatoes

Since some of the best grapes and the best tomatoes are harvested at the same time, at the end of September, it only makes sense to use both in a simple dish that will show off their flavors to the fullest. I use cherry tomatoes in this dish, sweet 100's when I can get them, which are so sweet I sometimes serve them to my wife for dessert. Finish the dish with a drizzle of the real stuff—real balsamic vinegar (see Sources, page 237). Or, if you don't want to spend the money, just use your everyday balsamic, but reduce it by half in a saucepan on the stove . **Serves 4**

2 ounces extra-virgin olive oil

1 pint cherry tomatoes

Salt

Freshly ground black pepper

1 medium bunch grapes (Muscat or Thompson), stemmed and halved

1/4 cup mint leaves

1 1/2 cups Wondra (see Note, page 140)

1 cup cornstarch

1 cup whole milk

Four 6-ounce skate wings

1/2 cup canola oil

3 tablespoons unsalted butter

Aceto balsamico (aged balsamic vinegar), for drizzling

Over a medium-high flame, heat the olive oil in a large sauté pan until hot but not smoking. Add the cherry tomatoes and 1/2 teaspoon each salt and pepper. Sauté until the tomatoes begin to crack and break down, 2 to 3 minutes. Add the grapes and continue to sauté until they begin to shrink, about 2 minutes. Transfer to a bowl, add the mint leaves, and toss to combine.

Set two wide shallow bowls near the stove. In one, combine the flour and the cornstarch, and season with 1 teaspoon each salt and pepper; pour the milk into the other bowl. Dip each skate wing into the milk, then lightly dredge in the flour mixture. Repeat with another dip in the milk and a final dredging of the flour. When all the skate wings have been dredged, set aside.

Heat the canola oil over a high flame until hot but not smoking. Add the butter. When the foam subsides, add the reserved skate wings. As they sizzle, carefully use your fingertips to press them down, giving them full contact with the pan. After 2 minutes, give them a quarter turn to the right. Cook until golden brown, about 3 minute per side (turn the skate carefully so it doesn't break apart). Transfer the cooked wings to a paper-towel-lined plate and season with salt and pepper.

Serve the skate with a heap of the sautéed tomatoes and grapes alongside, drizzled with a top-quality *balsamico.*

Crustaceans, Tentacles, Etc.

Shrimp
a la Plancha
with Fava Bean Puree

A la plancha is a Spanish preparation. I've never been to Spain, but I'm dying to go. A plancha is essentially a hot iron griddle that cooks things quickly while sealing in the flavor. I first ate this dish in a little restaurant in Trieste, where they call this preparation *a la prostra*, with broken oil and a puree of fava beans. Substitute white beans when fava beans are not in season (spring). Use a cast-iron frypan whenever you are making anything *a la plancha*. Or any frypan that can get really, really hot. **Serves 4**

2 pounds fresh fava beans, shelled

Sea salt

Freshly ground black pepper

1 pound medium white shrimp, shells on, split down the back, vein removed

3 tablespoons extra-virgin olive oil, plus high-quality extra-virgin olive oil, for drizzling

2 cloves garlic, crushed with the flat of a knife blade

Bring a large pot of salted water to a boil. Add the fava beans and cook until very tender, 4 or 5 minutes. Drain the favas in a colander, reserving 1/2 cup or so of the cooking water. Remove the outer skin from each fava. Transfer the beans and most of the reserved water to a food processor and pulse until nearly smooth. Add 1/2 teaspoon salt and 1/2 teaspoon pepper. Pulse until smooth. If the puree is still lumpy, add a drizzle more of the cooking water to smooth it out.

Season the shrimp with salt and pepper. Over a medium flame, heat the olive oil in a large, cast-iron skillet until hot but not smoking. Add the garlic and cook until softened, about 2 minutes. Add the shrimp, in two batches, if necessary, and cook for about 3 minutes per side. The shells should be pink and the flesh opaque.

To serve, spoon about 1/2 cup of the fava puree onto each of four serving plates. Drape the grilled shrimp across the puree, and then finish with a sprinkling of salt and freshly ground black pepper, and a drizzle of high-quality extra-virgin olive oil.

Grilled Shrimp
with Pancetta and Radicchio

I love the combination of grilled radicchio—which is simultaneously smoky and bitter—with meaty shrimp and smoky, porky pancetta (cured Italian bacon). But what really makes this dish is the *aceto balsamico*, which lends the whole affair a sweet, tangy finishing touch. **Serves 4**

1½ pounds medium shrimp, shells on, split down the back, vein removed

Sea salt

Freshly ground black pepper

¼ cup extra-virgin olive oil, plus high-quality extra-virgin olive oil, for drizzling

½ pound pancetta, cut into ½-inch lardons

1 clove garlic, thinly sliced

1 medium head radicchio, cut into 4 wedges

2 tablespoons *aceto balsamico* (aged balsamic vinegar)

Season the shrimp with salt and pepper. Heat 3 tablespoons of the olive oil in a large, straight-sided sauté pan until hot but not smoking. Add the shrimp, in two batches if necessary, and cook for about 3 minutes per side. (Add the remaining tablespoon of oil to the pan between batches if necessary.) The shells should be pink and the flesh opaque. Transfer the cooked shrimp to a plate and set aside.

Wipe the pan clean with a paper towel and add the diced pancetta. Cook over a medium flame until the fat begins to render, about 3 minutes. Add the garlic, stir to combine, and continue to cook until the lardons are browned and the garlic has softened, about 3 more minutes. Add the radicchio and the balsamic vinegar and continue to cook until the radicchio is tender and the vinegar has reduced slightly, 4 to 5 minutes.

To serve, spoon the wilted radicchio equally onto four serving plates. Top with the sautéed shrimp and drizzle with high-quality extra-virgin olive oil.

Scallops with Sicilian-Style Romanesco Broccoli

Scallops just happen to go really well with the Sicilian-Style Romanesco Broccoli. Romanesco broccoli is becoming increasingly popular. People like its firm texture and earthy flavor. Here's my prediction: Romanesco broccoli will become the next big vegetable. The nutty scallops accent the tangy sweetness of the broccoli. Come to think of it, I could eat this broccoli preparation with just about any kind of seafood. **Serves 4**

2 tablespoons pine nuts

5 tablespoons extra-virgin olive oil

1 small yellow onion, finely diced (about 1/2 cup)

1 tablespoon capers, drained

2 tablespoons white raisins

1/4 cup dry white wine

1 head Romanesco broccoli, halved and separated into florets

Sea salt

Freshly ground black pepper

Leaves of 4 sprigs flat-leaf parsley

1 pound sea scallops (about 12)

3 tablespoons unsalted butter, broken into 12 pieces

Preheat the oven to 300°F. Place the nuts in a shallow baking dish and toast them in the oven for 2 minutes (they burn quickly). Set aside.

Heat 2 tablespoons olive oil in a straight-sided sauté pan over a medium flame until hot but not smoking. Add the onion and cook until softened, about 7 minutes, stirring occasionally. Add the capers and raisins, followed by the wine. Stir to coat the ingredients, and cook for about 2 minutes, so the raisins can absorb the wine.

Add the broccoli florets along with 1/2 cup water. Season with 1/2 teaspoon each salt and pepper. The liquid in the pan should be gently bubbling; adjust the heat if necessary. Cover the pan, leaving a slight opening. Cook the broccoli until tender, 20 to 25 minutes, stirring frequently and monitoring the liquid in the pan: if it bubbles away entirely, add a tablespoon or two more water. Taste the broccoli to test for tenderness. Remove from the heat and set aside.

Dry the scallops with paper towels and season both sides with salt and pepper.

Heat the remaining 3 tablespoons olive oil in a large, preferably nonstick, sauté pan over a medium-high flame until smoking. Place the scallops in the pan, top each with a piece of butter, and cook, undisturbed, for about 3 minutes before turning them (they should caramelize on each side to a crisp golden brown).

Divide the scallops among four plates and serve with the delicious broccoli alongside.

Scallops

with Sautéed Spinach and Roasted Parsnips

I use parsnips a lot in my cooking—maybe it's because *pasternack* is Russian for parsnip. This dish is one of those seasonal bits of perfection that can't be improved upon. I love what the orange does to the parsnips—namely, brings a little sweet acidity and zesty flavor to them. You can use bay scallops if you can find them, or sea scallops that haven't been treated (called dry scallops; see page 64). **Serves 4**

1 pound large bay or dry scallops (about 12)

Sea salt

Freshly ground black pepper

4 to 5 tablespoons extra-virgin olive oil, plus high-quality extra-virgin olive oil, for drizzling

Sautéed Spinach (page 180)

Roasted Parsnips (recipe follows)

Dry the scallops with paper towels and season both sides with salt and pepper.

Heat 3 tablespoons olive oil over a medium-high flame in a large, preferably nonstick, sauté pan until smoking. Put one scallop in the pan to test if it's hot enough—the scallop should sizzle. Adjust heat if necessary and sauté them, in batches if ncessary. Cook, undisturbed, for 3 to 4 minutes before turning them (they should caramelize on each side to a crisp golden brown). Add 1 or 2 tablespoons oil to the pan between batches, if necessary. When the scallops are done, transfer them to a plate. Set aside.

Combine the Sautéed Spinach and Roasted Parsnips in a mixing bowl. Divide the mixture among four serving plates and top each with three scallops. Drizzle each plate lightly with a high-quality extra-virgin olive oil, a sprinkling of crunchy sea salt, and a few turns of freshly ground black pepper. Serve immediately.

Roasted Parsnips Serves 4

1½ pounds parsnips, peeled, root ends trimmed, and cut into 2-inch chunks

3 tablespoons extra-virgin olive oil

Sea salt

Freshly ground black pepper

2 tablespoons unsalted butter, at room temperature

Preheat the oven to 400°F.

Place the parsnips on a baking sheet and toss with the olive oil. Season with salt and pepper and roast until the parsnips are easily pierced with the tip of a knife, about 45 minutes.

When the parsnips are tender, remove from the oven and toss with the softened butter. Season with salt and pepper. The parsnips can be made ahead and reheated in a microwave.

Mussels
in the Style of Livorno

Livorno is a coastal town in southern Tuscany that has great olives and olive oil. I've spent a fair amount of time there and in the adjoining Cinque Terre, a series of connected seaside towns most easily navigated on foot. Cooks there prepare many dishes with capers, black olives, and tomato in some form (either fresh or sauce), so that's what I use here. The mussels we find in this country are all farm-raised, so they've been cleaned and washed for us. Just make sure they're closed when you buy them. This dish is really easy, quick, and delicious. Serve it with a loaf of crusty bread to soak up the sauce. **Serves 4**

3 tablespoons extra-virgin olive oil

2 cloves garlic, roughly chopped

2 whole peperoncino

**3 tablespoons capers
(preferably salt-packed), rinsed**

¼ cup pitted Gaeta olives

1 cup Basic Tomato Sauce (page 81)

Freshly ground black pepper

1 pound mussels

2 tablespoons roughly chopped basil leaves

2 tablespoons roughly chopped flat-leaf parsley

In a saucepan with a tight-fitting lid, heat the olive oil over a medium flame for about 1 minute. Add the garlic, peperoncino, capers, and olives. Cook for about 4 minutes, until the garlic has softened and the peperoncino is tender.

Add the tomato sauce, season with pepper, stir to blend, then add the mussels. Cover and cook until the shells open (discard those that don't), about 2 minutes.

Remove the pot from the stove. Add the basil and parsley, and stir gently to combine. Divide the mussels among four serving bowls, being sure to include some of the sauce in each dish.

Scallops
with Asparagus and Sugar Snap Peas

I love the clean, crisp flavors of this quintessentially spring dish. Peas and asparagus are both spring crops, and together they create this great grassy flavor. Sautéing is the best cooking method to draw out the natural sugar of the scallops. There's a magic scallop moment you arrive at when you're cooking them, when they're just crisp enough and not yet rubbery. You'll notice that I cook the scallops in equal parts oil and butter: the oil allows you to cook the scallops over a high flame without burning, and the butter gives them a lovely flavor and color. Just make sure you don't add the butter until the scallops are in the pan, or it will burn. **Serves 4**

¼ cup plus 3 tablespoons olive oil

½ pound sugar snap peas

½ pound spring asparagus, woody stems removed, cut into 2-inch pieces

Herb Garden Vinaigrette (recipe follows)

1 pound sea scallops (about 12)

3 tablespoons unsalted butter, broken into 12 pieces

Sea salt

Freshly ground black pepper

Heat the ¼ cup olive oil in a large sauté pan until hot but not smoking. Add the sugar snap peas and asparagus and sauté until tender and bright, about 4 minutes. Transfer to a bowl and dress with the vinaigrette.

Dry the scallops with paper towels and season both sides with salt and pepper. Heat the remaining 3 tablespoons olive oil in a large, preferably nonstick, sauté pan over a medium-high flame until smoking. Place the scallops in the pan, top each with a piece of butter, and cook, undisturbed, for about 3 minutes before turning them (they should caramelize on each side to a crisp golden brown). Transfer the cooked scallops to a plate.

Divide the dressed asparagus and snap peas among four small serving plates. Top each with 3 scallops. Sprinkle a little salt and freshly ground pepper over each and serve immediately.

Herb Garden Vinaigrette Makes 1½ cups

½ cup extra-virgin olive oil

½ cup canola oil

¼ cup sherry vinegar

¼ cup finely chopped assorted herbs
   (dill, tarragon, rosemary)

Sea salt

Freshly ground black pepper

Whisk the oils into the vinegar slowly and then add the chopped herbs. Season with salt and pepper.

Grilled Octopus
with Stewed Corona Beans

Beans and octopus are a classic Italian combination. Corona beans are a giant white bean I like, but you can use cannellini or even canned chickpeas for this dish. When you simmer the octopus, put some wine corks in the pan; they help tenderize the octopus. But make sure you don't use any salt when you initially cook the octopus, because the salt toughens it. Octopus tastes best if you buy it fresh and throw it in the freezer for a day. Grilling the octopus crisps its tips, and crispy is just about always better in my book. **Serves 4**

FOR THE BEANS

2 cups dried corona beans, soaked overnight (see Preparation Note)

1 stalk celery, cut into 3 pieces

1 carrot, peeled and cut into 3 pieces

½ small white onion, roughly chopped

2 sprigs thyme

1 bay leaf

FOR THE OCTOPUS

1 octopus, about 2½ pounds, head on, cleaned

4 cloves garlic, peeled

1 stalk celery, cut into 3 pieces

1 carrot, peeled and cut into 3 pieces

½ small white onion, roughly chopped

1 bay leaf

¾ cup dry red wine

Zest and juice of 1 lemon

Leaves of 5 sprigs flat-leaf parsley (about ¼ cup)

⅓ cup extra-virgin olive oil, plus more for brushing

2 heads frisée, leaves separated and rinsed

½ small red onion, diced

Sea salt

Freshly ground black pepper

Sherry Vinaigrette (page 19)

4 sprigs rosemary

Rosemary Oil (page 34)

Preheat the oven to 300°F.

MAKE THE BEANS

Using an ovenproof Dutch oven, trace the diameter of the pot onto a piece of parchment paper. Then cut out the circle and set aside. Place the beans, celery, carrot, onion, thyme, and bay leaf in the pot and fill with enough water to cover by at least 2 inches. Bring to a boil over a high flame. Turn off the flame, lay the reserved parchment circle on the surface of the beans, and cover with the lid.

Transfer to the oven and gently simmer for about 1½ hours, until the beans are creamy and tender. If they boil, reduce the oven temperature.

continued

Set the cooked beans on the stove top to cool in their liquid. Remove and discard the carrot, celery, and onion. Then drain in a colander, discard the bay leaf, and rinse with cool water. These beans can be stored, covered, in the refrigerator overnight.

MAKE THE OCTOPUS

Place the octopus in a large stockpot with three of the garlic cloves, the celery, carrot, white onion, bay leaf, and wine. Add some wine corks (see headnote) and fill the pot with water. Bring to a boil over a high flame, then reduce the heat to a low, gentle simmer. Cook, uncovered, for 1 to 1$\frac{1}{2}$ hours, adding more water if necessary to keep the octopus covered. The octopus should be completely tender (the tip of a paring knife should easily cut through it). Drain the octopus and set aside to cool.

Thinly slice the remaining clove of garlic. In a large glass mixing bowl, combine the garlic with the lemon zest and juice, parsley, and the $\frac{1}{3}$ cup olive oil. Cut the tentacles from the head and cut the head in half. Add the octopus to the lemon-parsley mixture and toss to coat. Refrigerate for at least 2 hours or overnight.

Prepare a charcoal fire and heat the grill over it (or use a stove-top grill pan).

Meanwhile, combine the frisée, red onion, and beans in a large mixing bowl.

Remove the octopus from the marinade. Brush with olive oil and season with salt and pepper. Grill the octopus over white-hot coals for 4 to 6 minutes per side, enough time for grill marks to form. Transfer to a plate.

Dress the frisée and beans with the vinaigrette, using your hands to toss. Divide the salad among four serving plates. Put the grilled octopus into the mixing bowl and toss to coat with the dressing. Arrange the octopus on top of the salads and garnish with a sprig of rosemary and a drizzle of Rosemary Oil. Serve immediately.

PREPARATION NOTE

The beans can be made a day or two ahead and refrigerated. The octopus, after simmering for 1$\frac{1}{2}$ hours, has to sit in the marinade for at least 2 hours or overnight. My best advice is to cook the beans and simmer the octopus the day before you serve this.

INGREDIENT NOTE

When it comes to cooking octopus, suction cups rule. So make sure that when you buy octopus it has two rows of suckers. I can't understand why anyone would serve octopus without the suction cups. They get a nice char when you grill them, and they contain a ton of the octopus's unique flavor.

Soft Scrambled Eggs with Lump Crabmeat

People go crazy over this simple dish. And they always end up saying to themselves, "Hey, I can make this at home." I say you're right, so here goes. Try to get the freshest possible eggs with big yellow yolks. I use milk instead of cream, because cream makes the eggs too heavy to serve with the shellfish. The key to this dish is sautéing the seafood first and then adding the eggs to scramble them in the same pan. This dish can also be made with lobster or rock shrimp and it will come out just as delicious. **Serves 4**

3 jumbo or 4 large farm eggs
2 tablespoons whole milk
Sea salt
Freshly ground black pepper

3 tablespoons unsalted butter
**1/2 cup lump crabmeat,
    picked over for shells and cartilage**
High-quality extra-virgin olive oil, for drizzling

In a medium mixing bowl, lightly whisk the eggs and milk. Season with 1/2 teaspoon each salt and pepper.

Melt the butter in a medium, nonstick sauté pan over medium heat. When the foam subsides, add the crabmeat and reduce the flame to low. Lightly sauté until the crabmeat begins to brown, about 3 minutes. Add the egg mixture. Use a heatproof rubber spatula to almost constantly stir the eggs and crabmeat as they gently cook and form small curds, 5 to 6 minutes.

Spoon onto four salad-size plates, season with salt and pepper, and a light drizzle of high-quality extra-virgin olive oil.

Tommy **Crab**

My crab guy's name is Tommy Hart. Everyone calls him Tommy Crab. For the longest time I didn't even know his last name. I think of him as the Ed Norton of the crustacean world, because he works for the county Department of Water Works, just like the Art Carney character did on *The Honeymooners*. Tommy's a big, strong-looking guy. You wouldn't want to try to steal his crabs from his traps. He would put a hurtin' on you.

Tommy's the last of the Mohicans, one of the last crabmen left on Long Island. I guess that's because there aren't that many crabs in my local waters anymore. He works the bay every day, because his boss allows him to set his work schedule around the tides. In the spring and early summer, he traps soft-shell crabs, in the summer he traps the hard-shell blue-claw crabs, and in the late fall he traps eels.

Why do I buy from Tommy Crab, even though I have to send my guy out to Tommy's garage in Long Island to pick up crabs and eels? Because his crabs are my neighbors, so I'm buying as local as I can, literally from around the corner. I'm not buying crabs from Maryland or Delaware, which is where most of the crabs you can buy in New York City come from.

Plus, Tommy's crabs taste better. They're sweeter, meatier, and bigger than other crabs. The other day I ate two of Tommy's soft-shells at my friend Artie's restaurant. Together they weighed one pound, four ounces. Those were two humongous crabs. Sometimes I make a pasta sauce of cooked-down Tommy crabs, canned cherry tomatoes, whole garlic cloves, one cherry pepper, and a little brandy. Although my customers look at it and wonder where all the crab is, once they taste it they realize most of the crabmeat and shell has been cooked down into the sauce, and they get a supremely intense crab-flavor hit in every bite.

Tommy's favorite season is Christmas, because at Esca we serve a traditional Neapolitan seven-fish dinner featuring fried eels. Sometimes Tommy will catch eels in November in a special trap that keeps them until mid-December when he can sell them for a lot more money. If those eels would be worth a dollar a pound in November, they're going to be worth seven dollars a pound come Christmas. Smart businessman, that Tommy Crab.

Fried Soft-Shell Crabs
with Ramps

I'm very particular whom I buy my soft-shell crabs from, and you should be, too. I get mine from Tommy Crab (see page 228). When you buy soft-shell crabs they shouldn't be moving around. Their backs should feel soft, like a baby's bottom. I like soft-shells fried, as they are here, or grilled. When I've sautéed them, too often they've come out oily. **Serves 4**

8 medium or 10 small young ramps

½ cup plus 3 tablespoons extra-virgin olive oil

2 cloves garlic, thinly sliced

Sea salt

Freshly ground black pepper

1½ cups Wondra (see Note, page 140)

1 cup cornstarch

1 cup whole milk

8 small to medium soft-shell crabs, cleaned by your fishmonger

1 lemon, thinly sliced

Sherry Vinaigrette (page 19)

Clean the ramps by cutting off the root ends, and cutting away the top leaves, leaving just a bit of green. Rinse under cool running water and then dry. Cut them into ¼-inch pieces.

Heat 3 tablespoons of the olive oil in a straight-sided sauté pan over medium-high heat until hot but not smoking. Add the garlic and ramps and sauté until the ramps are tender, 3 to 5 minutes (the cooking time will increase as ramp season progresses and they grow firmer). Use a slotted spoon to transfer the ramps to a bowl, and season with salt and pepper; keep warm. Discard the garlic and the oil.

In a wide shallow bowl, combine the flour with the cornstarch and season with 1 teaspoon each salt and pepper. Whisk to combine. Place the milk in another shallow bowl.

Wipe the sauté pan clean with a paper towel. Add the ½ cup oil and heat over a medium-high flame until very hot.

Dip the crabs into the milk, and then dredge lightly in the flour mixture. Shake off the excess flour, and then repeat: soak in the milk, dredge in the flour, shake. Repeat with the lemon slices. Place the crabs in the sauté pan, top side down, along with the lemon slices—they should sizzle. Cook the crabs until they are golden brown, about 3 minutes per side. Transfer the cooked crabs to a paper-towel-lined plate to cool, and season immediately with a sprinkling of salt and freshly ground black pepper.

Set out four serving plates. Drizzle the vinaigrette around each plate and place two crabs, some ramps, and a few lemon slices on each. Serve immediately.

Baked Clams
with Italian-Style Bread Crumbs and Horseradish

Growing up on Long Island, near the water and lots of southern Italian restaurants, I'm a huge fan of traditional baked clams done right and I had dozens of delicious baked clams at King Umberto's in Elmont. I use steamers (also known as mud clams) and homemade bread crumbs, and I give the clams a little jolt with the fresh horseradish. You have to cook the garlic in the bread crumbs or you'll end up with the raw garlicky flavor that ruins many a plate of baked clams. The key to these clams is saving the clam liquor when you shuck them. Adding it in later is what gives these clams their wonderfully intense clam flavor. **Serves 4**

12 littleneck or cherrystone clams,
    shucked, juice reserved

Extra-virgin olive oil

¼ cup freshly grated horseradish

1 cup Italian-Style Bread Crumbs
    (recipe follows)

1 lemon, halved

Sea salt

Freshly ground black pepper

Preheat the broiler.

Spread the clams in their half shells on a baking sheet. Drizzle each with a drop or two of extra-virgin olive oil.

In a small mixing bowl, combine the horseradish and the bread crumbs. Cover each clam with a hefty pinch of the bread-crumb-horseradish mixture. Lightly pat it down. Cut one of the lemon halves into four wedges. Then use the other half lemon to put a drop or two of juice on each clam. Drizzle the clams lightly with the extra-virgin olive oil and put them under the broiler. Cook for about 6 minutes, drizzling each with the reserved clam juice halfway through, until the bread crumbs are lightly golden and bubbly. Transfer to a serving plate, sprinkle with a little salt and freshly ground pepper, and serve immediately with the lemon wedges alongside.

Italian-Style Bread Crumbs Makes 2 cups

I know you can buy decent bread crumbs these days at the grocery store, but they won't taste half as good as these.

1 loaf Italian bread

1½ tablespoons extra-virgin olive oil

1 teaspoon finely diced garlic

1 tablespoon lemon zest

1½ tablespoons chopped parsley

2 teaspoons sea salt

1 teaspoon freshly ground black pepper

Preheat the oven to 350°F.

Tear the loaf of bread into chunks, say, 2 inches long. Place them on a baking sheet. Bake until the bread is dry and crunchy, about 15 minutes. Put the chunks in a food processor and pulse to a fine crumb. Set aside.

Heat 1 tablespoon of the olive oil in a small sauté pan. Add the garlic and stir until it begins to brown, about 3 minutes. Add the lemon zest and cook for 30 seconds, until fragrant. Add the bread crumbs, parsley, and the remaining ½ tablespoon olive oil, and stir well. Season with salt and pepper and remove from the heat. The bread crumbs can be stored in a covered container until ready to use.

Sources

Most of the food you need to cook the recipes in this book is available at your local fishmonger, farmers' market, or any good grocery store. However, there are a few ingredients that may be hard to find. I have noted them in the text, and you will find online and/or mail-order sources for them here.

Most of the hard-to-find Italian items are available online at Gustiamo.com or via mail or phone order from Di Palo Fine Foods in New York. Louis Di Palo's family has been making mozzarella and selling great Italian foods for almost a hundred years in New York's Little Italy. Louis has forgotten more about Italian foodstuffs than I'll ever remember. He will take orders over the phone and ship anything he sells in his tiny store, but he doesn't have a catalogue or a Web site. That's okay, because when you place your order you will speak to Louis himself, and he will gladly answer any questions you might have. Just don't plan on a brief conversation. Louis likes to talk, but that's not a bad thing. He has a lot to say.

For preserved mackerel (page 2), Recca brand anchovies (page 5), jarred or canned ventresca tuna (page 21), mozzarella di bufala (page 36 and others), bigoli (page 94), Sicilian olive oil or any other high-quality extra-virgin olive oil (throughout the book, for drizzling), Sicilian sea salt (throughout the book), canned cherry tomatoes or puree (page 37), and French or Italian feta (page 90; Di Palo only):

Di Palo Fine Foods: 200 Grand Street, New York, NY 10013, Tel.: 212-226-1033

Gustiamo: 718-860-2949 or www.gustiamo.com

For stoneground polenta (page 155):
803-467-4122 or www.ansonmills.com

For baccalà (page 10) and all types of fish needed to make crudo (starting on page 43):
800-944-7848 or www.browne-trading.com

For scungilli (page 7):
Don's Seafood: 717-845-6830, 717-873-4191, or www.dons-seafood.com

Acknowledgments

Dave Pasternack would like to thank his co-author Ed Levine, who thought I had something to say and helped me say it; Kathryn Kelling, who was able to take my illegible recipes on tattered pieces of paper and turn them into what you see before you; Vicky Bijur, agent extraordinaire, who pushed all the right buttons and kept the wolf-fish from our door; Chris Pavone at Artisan, who kept us on track recipe by recipe, page by page; Mario Batali, Joe Bastianich, and Simon Dean, my partners, who helped make my dream of a seafood restaurant not just about salmon, swordfish, and tuna come true; my kitchen staff at Esca past and present, who do a lot of hard work that allows me to take the credit. The entire front-of-the-house staff at Esca, who really make me look good every day and night. My parents, who put a fishing rod and a fry pan in my hand before I could walk. And of course my darlings Donna and Ruby, the lights of my life.

Ed Levine would like to thank Kathryn Kellinger, recipe tester and contributor in so many unacknowledged ways; Dave Pasternack, fisherman, chef, father, husband, and friend, who taught me enough about fish and life in the last few years that even I was able to catch a striped bass; my wife and agent Vicky Bijur, who proved when I met her that there were just enough fish in the sea; our editor, Chris Pavone, at Artisan, who edited and shepherded this book with uncommon clarity and forthrightness; Pam Cannon, who believed in our idea from the outset; Allyson Ehrie, an early recipe tester; Mario Batali and Joe Bastianich, who recognized that Dave's story had to be told. And my mom and dad, who are looking down from on high wondering how their landlubbing little boy ever ended up writing a book about fish and fishing.

Index

Y

yellowfin tuna, 13
Yellowtail with Spaghetti Squash, Oven-Dried
   Tomatoes, and Vin Cotto, 187

Z

Zucchini, Pan-Roasted Cobia with Olives and, 168;
   illus., 169
Zucchini Blossoms Stuffed with Anchovies and
   Mozzarella, 36
Zuppe di Pesce Amalfitano, 39–40; illus., 38

About the Authors

When New York–born–and–bred chef **David Pasternack** is not in the kitchen of Esca, his seafood mecca, he can be found fishing in the Atlantic—from the Rockaways to Montauk Point. He is the winner of the James Beard Foundation award for best New York City chef and has been known to bring his catch of the day into the city via the Long Island Rail Road. Prior to opening Esca, Dave worked in the kitchens of Bouley and Picholine. He lives in Long Beach with his wife, Donna Peltz, and their daughter, Ruby. This is his first book.

Co-author **Ed Levine** is a frequent contributor to *The New York Times* and SeriousEats.com, a Web site with fresh video, blogs, and conversation that is home base for passionate, discerning eaters on the Internet. He is the author of *Pizza: A Slice of Heaven*, *New York Eats*, and *New York Eats (More)*, as well as a radio and television producer and host whose shows have been nominated for James Beard Foundation awards four years in a row. He lives in New York City with his wife, Vicky Bijur.